THE FUTURE OF CHRISTIANITY

CAC Publishing

Center for Action and Contemplation

cac.org

"*Oneing*" is an old English word that was used by Lady Julian of Norwich (1342–1416) to describe the encounter between God and the soul. The Center for Action and Contemplation proudly borrows the word to express the divine unity that stands behind all of the divisions, dichotomies, and dualisms in the world. We pray and publish with Jesus' words, "that all may be one" (John 17:21).

EDITOR:
Vanessa Guerin

ASSOCIATE EDITOR:
Shirin McArthur

PUBLISHER:
The Center for Action and Contemplation

ADVISORY BOARD:
David Benner
James Danaher
Ilia Delio, OSF
Sheryl Fullerton
Stephen Gaertner, OPraem
Ruth Patterson

Design and Composition by Nelson Kane

Oneing
An Alternative Orthodoxy

The biannual literary journal of the Center for Action and Contemplation.

The Perennial Tradition, Vol. 1, No. 1, Spring 2013

Ripening, Vol. 1, No. 2, Fall 2013

Transgression, Vol. 2, No. 1, Spring 2014

Evidence, Vol. 2, No. 2, Fall 2014

Emancipation, Vol. 3, No. 1, Spring 2015

Innocence, Vol. 3, No. 2, Fall 2015

Perfection, Vol. 4, No. 1, Spring 2016

Evolutionary Thinking, Vol. 4, No. 2, Fall 2016

Transformation, Vol. 5, No. 1, Spring 2017

Politics and Religion, Vol. 5, No. 2, Fall 2017

Anger, Vol. 6, No. 1, Spring 2018

Unity and Diversity, Vol. 6, No. 2, Fall 2018

The Universal Christ, Vol. 7, No. 1, Spring 2019

Oneing is a limited-edition publication; therefore, some editions are no longer in print. To order available editions of *Oneing*, please visit https://store.cac.org/.

Oneing

VOLUME 7 NO. 2

Amidst a time of planetary change and disruption, we envision a recovery of our deep connection to each other and our world, led by Christian and other spiritual movements that are freeing leaders and communities to overcome dehumanizing systems of oppression and cooperate in the transforming work of Love.
—Vision Statement, Center for Action and Contemplation

A T THE CENTER for Action and Contemplation, the entire team has committed to in-depth work with Race, Equity, and Belonging (REB)—a process which is opening our hearts and minds to greater awareness of global disparity. It is transformative work that is palpably shifting the culture of the CAC in order for us to do what is ours to do in the world.

The REB work has offered us a new lens through which to view and incorporate CAC's vision statement. Although it seems lofty, the vision statement is deeply rooted in the Franciscan alternative orthodoxy—a critical contribution to the future of Christianity—as we recognize and embrace the Christ in other traditions and cultures.

And yet, how can we even begin to imagine the future of Christianity without first recognizing how it has managed to sustain itself—for better or worse—for over two thousand years?

In "Loving the Church Back to Life," Shane Claiborne states it well:

> Just as we critique the worst of the church, we should also celebrate her at her best. We need to mine the fields of church history and find the treasures, the gems. We need to celebrate the best that each tradition can bring—I want the fire of the Pentecostals,

the love of Scripture of the Lutherans, the political imagination of the Anabaptists, the roots of the Orthodox, the mystery of the Catholics, and the zeal of the evangelicals.

In her article, "The Future of Christianity," Native American Christian mystic, activist, and author Kaitlin Curtice writes of the liberating process of releasing elements of the Christian tradition. Of the Potawatomi tribe, Kaitlin grew up in a fundamentalist, evangelical Christian denomination. In order to give herself and her children an opportunity to engage with a non-legalistic, nondual faith experience, she had to deconstruct and decolonize the faith tradition within which she was raised. This challenging process transformed the way she experiences and lives within the Christian tradition. Kaitlin writes:

> The future of Christianity is one that fully envelops all that we are as people in this process, so that we come to know ourselves and those around us, so that we know why it is important to be people who seek justice for the earth, for our creature kin on the earth, and for our human kin around us.

We are reminded of this by Roman Catholic Archbishop John Wester in his article, "Abide in Me: The Church's Love Affair with Christ," when he writes, "The Church is one because Christ is always at the center. Christ came to gather us together, to break down the walls that divide us, and to restore unity.... Thus, the Church is always about the business of 'making one.'"

As we become more aware of the evolution of the church into this sacred oneness, we are able to look beyond the confining human-built edifices that separate us from Christ's loving presence in all that is created, or, as Richard Rohr states so eloquently in "Powering Down: The Future of Institutions,"

> Most people today, in fact, understand church to mean a building, rather than where "two or three gather in [Jesus'] name," where the Divine Presence is promised just as certainly as it is promised in the bread, in the Bible, in the Sacraments, or in any anointed leadership: "I am in your midst" (Matthew 18:20).

While we at CAC know that we don't have all the answers, we are aware that the change we wish to see in the world must begin with us. Therefore, we rely both on our vision statement above and our mission statement below to remind us of the life-altering work required to inspire and empower us into thinking beyond CAC, so as to:

> Open the door for a critical mass of spiritual seekers to experience the transformative wisdom of the Christian contemplative tradition and nurture its emergence in service to the healing of our world.

I would suggest that most of the contributors to this edition of *Oneing* would agree with Diarmuid O'Murchu, as he states in "Christianity's Future: An Evolutionary Perspective," that "Christianity is undergoing a huge evolutionary shift, marking the decline—and eventual death—of the imperial paradigm." However, each brings a surprising perspective, in the spirit of the CAC's vision and mission statements, to the challenging concept of engaging an unknowable future for a church with a very long history.

Vanessa Guerin
Editor

CONTRIBUTORS

KAITLIN B. CURTICE, an enrolled citizen of the Potawatomi Citizen Band Nation, is a Native American Christian mystic, writer, speaker, and blogger. She is the author of *Glory Happening: Finding the Divine in Everyday Places*, a collection of fifty essays and prayers. Kaitlin writes words of remembrance and testimony, words about the connectedness of humanity and what God teaches us through each other and ourselves. She has contributed to *OnBeing, Decaturish, Ruminate Magazine, The Mudroom, Relevant Magazine Online, Sojourners*, and *CBE International*. To learn more about Kaitlin Curtice, please visit https://kaitlincurtice.com/.

DIARMUID O'MURCHU, MSC, a member of the Sacred Heart Missionary Order, is a social psychologist whose working life has mostly involved social ministry, predominantly in London, UK. He has worked as a couples' counsellor, in bereavement work, AIDS-HIV counselling, and with homeless people and refugees. As a workshop leader and group facilitator focusing on adult faith development, Diarmuid has worked in Europe, USA, Canada, Australia, The Philippines, Thailand, India, Peru, and several African countries. He is the author of numerous books, including *Quantum Theology: Spiritual Implications of the New Physics, In the Beginning Was the Spirit: Science, Religion, and Indigenous Spirituality*, and *On Being a Postcolonial Christian: Embracing an Empowering Faith*. To learn more about Diarmuid O'Murchu, visit www.diarmuid13.com.

ARCHBISHOP JOHN CHARLES WESTER is an American prelate of the Catholic Church, the twelfth Archbishop of the Archdiocese of Santa Fe. He was ordained in 1976 after twelve years in seminary and became a priest in his native San Francisco. Pope John Paul II appointed him titular Bishop of Lamiggiga and auxiliary bishop for the Archdiocese of San Francisco in 1998. In 2007, he was appointed by Pope Benedict XVI the ninth bishop of the Diocese of Salt Lake City. On April 27, 2015, Archbishop Wester was appointed by Pope Francis as the twelfth Archbishop of Santa Fe. To learn more about Archbishop Wester, please visit https://archdiosf.org/about-archbishop-wester.

RICHARD ROHR, OFM, is a Franciscan priest of the New Mexico Province and the Founding Director of the Center for Action and Contemplation in Albuquerque, New Mexico. An internationally recognized author and spiritual leader, Fr. Richard teaches primarily on incarnational mysticism, non-dual consciousness, and contemplation, with a particular emphasis on how these affect the social justice issues of our time. Along with many recorded conferences, he is the author of numerous books, including his newest, *The Universal Christ: How a Forgotten Reality Can Change Everything We See, Hope For, and Believe*. To learn more about Fr. Richard Rohr and the CAC, visit https://cac.org/richard-rohr/richard-rohr-ofm/.

DIANA BUTLER BASS, PhD, is an historian of Christianity and a popular speaker, teacher, and preacher in a variety of venues in the United States and internationally. Her bylines include *The Washington Post*, *The New York Times Syndicate*, and *The Huffington Post*. Diana has commented widely in the media on religion, politics, and culture and has written numerous books, including *Grounded: Finding God in the World—A Spiritual Revolution*, *Christianity After Religion: The End of Church and the Birth of a New Spiritual Awakening*, and *Christianity for the Rest of Us: How the Neighborhood Church Is Transforming the Faith*. To learn more about Diana Butler Bass, please visit http://dianabutlerbass.com/.

SHANE CLAIBORNE is a best-selling author, renowned activist, sought-after speaker, and self-proclaimed "recovering sinner." Shane writes and speaks around the world about peacemaking, social justice, and Jesus, and is the author of several books, including *The Irresistible Revolution: Living as an Ordinary Radical* and his newest, *Executing Grace: How the Death Penalty Killed Jesus and Why It's Killing Us*. He is the visionary leader of The Simple Way in Philadelphia and co-director of Red Letter Christians. His work has been featured on Fox News, NPR, and CNN, and he has written for multiple publications, including *Esquire*, *SPIN*, and *The Wall Street Journal*. To learn more about Shane Claiborne, please visit http://www.shaneclaiborne.com/.

BRIAN D. McLAREN is an author, speaker, activist, and public theologian. A former college English teacher and pastor, he is a passionate advocate for "a new kind of Christianity"—just, generous, and working with people of all faiths for the common good. Brian is a faculty member of The Center for Action and Contemplation's Living School and is the author of numerous books. His most recent joint project is an illustrated children's book (for all ages) titled *Cory and the Seventh Story*, and his upcoming writing projects include *The Galapagos Islands: A Spiritual Journey* (Fall 2019), *Faith After Doubt* (Spring 2021), and *Do I Stay Christian?* (Spring 2022). To learn more about Brian McLaren, please visit http://brianmclaren.net/.

Rev. Canon Nontombi Naomi Tutu, a human rights activist, was born in South Africa and has also lived in Lesotho, the United Kingdom, and the United States. She has divided her adult life between South Africa and the United States. The daughter of Archbishop Desmond Tutu, Rev. Tutu is an ordained priest in the Episcopal Church. She is a sought-after speaker and consultant, and the recipient of four honorary doctorates from universities and colleges in the US and Nigeria. Rev. Tutu is a collaborator on a forthcoming book provisionally titled *I Don't Think of You as Black: Honest Conversations on Race and Racism*. To learn more about Naomi Tutu, please visit https://www.allamericanspeakers.com/speakers/399205/Naomi-Tutu.

Wesley Granberg-Michaelson served as General Secretary of the Reformed Church in America from 1994 to 2011. Previously he was Director of Church and Society at the World Council of Churches in Geneva, the Associate Editor of *Sojourners* Magazine, and Executive and Legislative Assistant to United States Senator Mark Hatfield. He is the author of seven books, including *Future Faith: Ten Challenges Reshaping Christianity in the 21st Century*, *From Times Square to Timbuktu: The Post-Christian West Meets the Non-Western Church* and *Unexpected Destinations: An Evangelical Pilgrimage to World Christianity*. His numerous articles have appeared in *Sojourners*, *Christian Century*, *Christianity Today*, *The Church Herald*, *Ecumenical Review*, and other publications. To learn more about Wes Granberg-Michaelson, visit https://sojo.net/biography/wesley-granberg-michaelson.

Shirin McArthur, MDiv, is a spiritual guide, editor, writer, and poet who lives in Arizona. She is a former CAC staff member and the Associate Editor of *Oneing*. She is a regular contributor to the Liturgical Press *Loose Leaf Lectionary*, leads online and in-person retreats, and is a contemplative photographer. Shirin's award-winning blog is part of the Christian Century network. To read her blog and learn more about Shirin McArthur, visit https://shirinmcarthur.com/.

Lee Staman, MLIS, is the Systems Librarian at the Center for Action and Contemplation. Currently his work is focused on cataloging everything Richard Rohr has said and written. He has a passion for the role of information and technology in the modern world along with a deep interest in the history of religious thought. Lee has degrees in philosophy and theology and resides in Seattle, Washington with his wife and two children, to whom he reads the Patristics to put them to sleep. Lee Staman may be contacted at lstaman@cac.org.

On the Mystery of the Incarnation

It's when we face for a moment
the worst our kind can do, and shudder to know
the taint in our own selves, that awe
cracks the mind's shell and enters the heart:
not to a flower, not to a dolphin,
to no innocent form
but to this creature vainly sure
it and no other is god-like, God
(out of compassion for our ugly
failure to evolve) entrusts,
as guest, as brother,
the Word.

—Denise Levertov[1]

The Future of Christianity

By Kaitlin B. Curtice

There's no one among us who hasn't been floored by something unexpected, new or strange. All of us have been touched by the wondrous in something simple or common: the gleam of a dragonfly wing in the sunshine, the whirr of a hummingbird, the haunting call of a bird in the dark.

—Richard Wagamese, *One Story, One Song*

C HRISTIANITY, LIKE EVERY other religion in the world, was born out of the desire for people to understand something of God, of Sacredness, of Belonging, of Mystery.

I grew up in Southern Baptist evangelical Christianity, a sect of Christianity that is rooted in fundamentalism, legalism, and the idea that, at the end of the day, what we need most is to pray the sinner's prayer and secure for ourselves and those around us a spot in heaven. It is a religion of complete duality: *us* versus *them*, *light* versus *dark*, *in* versus *out*. Because of this duality, it holds little space for grace, for mystery, or for questions.

After I had children, those questions began to emerge from within me, including questions about who I am as a Potawatomi woman living in America. If I wanted my children to have a faith that has room for all of who they are, didn't I want the same for myself? So, I began deconstructing and decolonizing my faith, a process that brought both grief and healing.

When I think of what the church will look like in the coming years, I think about people who are seekers and questioners. I'm looking around America at colonized white churches that hold no place for those who are on the margins; for Black, Indigenous, or other people of color; for women; for people with disabilities; for LGBTQIA+ people.

While the Southern Baptist faith was born in the United States, it is a colonizing force that has rooted itself across the world through missionary exploits. What might the future of Christianity look like when this is part of what we've given to those around us and around the world?

Even though not all of Christianity is based on ideas of colonization, much of it is, and, because there is no way to *go back*, we have to ask today what it might mean to repair and to decolonize, when and where we can.

I believe the future of colonized Christianity in America must be one that *embraces its grief and questions*.

That's probably the last thing you and I want to hear, but, of all the things I think the church needs, it's space to truly grieve.

We need space to grieve the actual oppressive systems we ourselves have created and sustained.

We need space to grieve our own loss and actually *bear it together*.

We need space to grieve that the Christianity we've inherited today does not reflect the universal Christ.

In May of this year, one of my dear friends, Rachel Held Evans (1981–2019), a prolific writer and leader in the church, passed away suddenly. A few months later, I was in Cape Cod, Massachusetts recording the audio for my first book. In the midst of my grief, I was

We need space to grieve the actual oppressive systems we ourselves have created and sustained.

working on something deeply meaningful to me and, over the course of a few days, I found myself opened up to that grief, but also to laughter, to joy, to stillness, to pain, and to the wideness of Sacred Mystery. The grief made way for me to notice things I hadn't noticed before, like the way the wind by the ocean carries a voice all its own that quieted mine as I ached.

The grief led me deeper into myself, deeper into knowing the world around me. It is the same need that is waiting for all of us, so that we may, together, enter into our collective grief, into mourning, so that we find we are opened up to the wonder and love that inhabits the world around us.

America's collective conscience, and so the conscience of the church, is struggling right now to understand its position in the world and in history. Are we people and institutions made up of love, or are we people and institutions that continue cycles of hate?

To deeply and honestly ask these questions, we often turn to our prophets. The prophets of our day are not the ones who are proclaiming that everything is fine. The prophets have always been the ones on the street corner reminding us that we do not value everyone as we should; they are the community leaders calling us back to the land again and forcing us to look straight into injustice; they are children and women who are abused and looking for safety.

The prophets are the ones who lament, and who lead us out of that lament. *They are the ones who grieve.*

As has been the case throughout history, we see the oppressed rise up and protest injustices around the world. Indigenous activists gather to protect the earth from destruction and citizens gather to speak up against corrupt governments. This is holy work, born from that same desire to know what is sacred in the world and protect it.

Protest is grief in motion. It is proclaiming out loud that things are not as they should be and asking what needs to happen for things to change.

White American evangelical Christianity needs to take itself through the grieving process, through the work of protesting those things that are not right. This will ultimately end in transformation. When we circle back to understanding our place in the world, we acknowledge things like white supremacy, hatred, ableism, racism, and toxic masculinity.

Working through this grief will lead to de-centering whiteness and deconstructing oppressive systems, to centering and reconstructing by those who have not been heard for centuries.

The future of Christianity is one that fully envelops all that we are as people in this process, so that we come to know ourselves and those around us, so that we know why it is important to be people who seek justice for the earth, for our creature kin on the earth, and for our human kin around us.

In the epigraph, Ojibwe writer Richard Wagamese (1955–2017) described this idea of opening ourselves to wonder, engaging the world around us with all of our senses. Our children know how to do this better than anyone, and so they are always teaching us to open ourselves up. Mystics of any religion learn that to be human means to embrace our childlikeness, to understand what is holy in the world, including embracing our grief along the way.

Understanding what it means to be Potawatomi has been a full and difficult journey, because to know what it means to be Potawatomi is to come to terms with the fact that we have been colonized, oppressed, and assimilated in the name of Christianity, time and again throughout history, just as many Indigenous peoples have been, all over the world.

Because Indigenous identity is directly tied to the land, we grieve because the land grieves. We grieve because the water cannot run clean. We grieve because we know what has been stolen from us and

Because Indigenous identity is directly tied to the land, we grieve because the land grieves.

we are working to return to who we are. My questions and struggles with Christianity lead me to understand that the vast expanse of God is ever-widening, and I couldn't control it even if I tried.

That is the beauty of faith, of spirituality, of seeking.

THE POTAWATOMI FLOOD story is a perfect example of moving through grief to begin again, to ask what is next, to dream of a better future that is envisioned by sacred love.

In this story, the earth is completely flooded by Creator, Mamogosnan. Original Man, Wiske, spends his time resting on a large log with some of the animals surrounding him. After some time, he decides to try to rebuild the earth again. The animals begin to dive down to the bottom of the water to try to gather dirt so they can create land again, but animal after animal fails. Finally, Zheshko the Muskrat offers to go. No one believes he can do it, but he dives down, all the way to the bottom of the water and comes up, lifeless, with a piece of dirt held in his paw. He does what he set out to do.

Turtle, Mshike, offers his shell as a starting place for the land. They place the dirt on the back of the turtle and the earth begins again. Life comes from the sacrifice of the muskrat.

This story is powerful because I can imagine Wiske sitting on that log for days, weeks, maybe months, grieving. He is grieving a world lost, grieving that things aren't as they should be. But, before he and the animals can dream of a new world, before they can begin to dive down into the water with hopes of coming up with dirt in their paws, they must go through that grief.

We move through our collective grief so that, one day, we can dream again; so that we can ask what life will look like on the other side.

Perhaps, right now, in Christianity, we are experiencing a flood. We are asking how things got to be this way, how a religion that is said to be based in love can be so riddled with white supremacy and colonialism and hate. So, we must grieve what we've lost, what's been broken. We must grieve long and hard before we can ask how to begin again.

After some time, the earth became as we see it today. Potawatomi people call this land Turtle Island because we honor Mshike for offering his shell to begin again. We honor the partnership of the muskrat and the turtle, who came together to dream of something beyond themselves.

That is what we must do today. We must lament, grieve, protest, wail, and wait.

We also hold on to the image of one day beginning again. We hold on to wonder and to one another. One day, those who come after us will understand the world as we never did. They will understand God and sacred belonging in ways we never could. I hope and dream for that.

> Words can only open the door, and we can only weep on the threshold of our incommunicable thirst after the incomprehensible.
>
> —Abraham Joshua Heschel

Christianity's Future:

An Evolutionary Perspective

By Diarmuid O'Murchu

C HRISTIANITY IS A world religion consisting of an estimated 1,400 denominations, the largest being Roman Catholicism, with an estimated membership of 1.2 billion people. Traditional Christian denominations, such as Catholicism, Protestantism, Methodism, Presbyterianism, and the Quakers, are often depicted as losing numbers and—much more—losing cultural impact as moral forces in society at large. The fastest growing denomination today is Pentecostalism, with an estimated 500 million members around the world; the Yoido Full Gospel Church in Seoul, South Korea comprises 800,000 members.

Christianity is a highly complex global movement, with an evolutionary impetus today that popular media grossly underestimate.

Media tend to judge Christianity by the obvious decline in one or another of its major denominations, leaving us with a partial and superficial analysis. There is certainly a crisis, not so much in terms of numbers or practice, but in terms of cultural identity and social influence. The crisis is not that of Christianity in itself, but of its articulation through the various denominations. The foundational problem is captured in the oft-cited quote erroneously attributed to Mahatma Gandhi (1869–1948): "I like your Christ; I do not like your Christians. Your Christians are so unlike your Christ."

AN EVOLUTIONARY PERSPECTIVE

As a social scientist, I feel we do greater justice to the complex landscape of contemporary Christianity by attending to some of the key evolutionary processes which impact every feature of our contemporary age. To spare the reader the technical elaboration of Darwinian evolution, I suggest the following schema, structured around three words: Growth – Change – Complexity.

Growth is a universal feature of all life and is easily observed throughout the organic world.

Change is the more subtle dynamic that drives and sustains meaningful growth. For instance, every cell in the human body dies and is reconstituted every seven years. It is more accurate to describe a human being as an evolving process rather than a stable, fixed product. Change also includes decay, decline, and death. Without such diminution, novelty cannot transpire and creativity is largely suppressed.

Complexity is the unpredictable ensemble through which each new form is enriched, forever requiring a deeper wisdom to comprehend the ensuing meaning. Such complexity is often characterized by paradox, such as the paradoxical mix of creation-and-destruction we observe throughout the entire creation.

One of the leading theorists on evolution today is Franciscan Sr. Ilia Delio, who captures the three features outlined above:

> Evolution is less a mechanism than a process—a constellation of law, chance, spontaneity, and deep time.... Evolution is not simply a biological mechanism of gene swapping or environmental pressures. It is the unfolding and development of consciousness

in which consciousness plays a significant role in the process of convergence and complexification. Evolution gives rise to religion when consciousness unfolds in a "Thou-embraced-I."[1]

CHRISTIANITY'S EVOLUTIONARY STORY

RARELY HAS EVOLUTION been employed in our understanding of Christianity. As Richard Rohr observes in his reflection on Catholicism, imperial power cast a shadow over the seminal vision, reminding us that more foundational truths still await a more discerning mode of retrieval. Patriarchal power was never meant to be a central feature of Christianity; empowerment was—and continues to be—its central driving force.

As an evolutionary story, Christianity did not begin about two thousand years ago. It makes more evolutionary sense to trace its origins to the emergence of the human species, some *seven million years ago.*[2] As an incarnational faith system, Christianity focuses on the body, particularly the human body. God's embodied presence in and through the human, or, to put it another way, the human face of God made radically visible on earth, first emerged with our human becoming some seven million years ago.

The ensuing evolutionary story is well-known today, thanks to the extensive research on human origins, which can be accessed through several webpages. It provides a fascinating, hope-filled narrative of which most humans are frighteningly ignorant. Because we remained very close to the natural world for most of that time, we actually flourished as a species, and, for most of the time, we got it right (because we remained very close to nature).

That unfolding narrative reached a high point—an axial moment—about ten thousand years ago, when humans, endowed

Patriarchal power was never meant to be a central feature of Christianity.

with a heightened sense of consciousness, embarked upon a new evolutionary phase, mistakenly called the Agricultural Revolution. Like previous high points, it is full of complexity, with a classical mixture of light and darkness. This is the evolutionary context out of which was born the great world religions, including Christianity.

JESUS AS THE CHRIST FIGURE

CENTRAL TO THE CHRISTIAN story is the person of Jesus, whose deeper meaning has been literalized to a degree that has seriously undermined the archetypal significance that Jesus represents.[3] As the Christ-archetype, Jesus is not merely a divine representative. First and foremost, he represents the human face of God made radically visible on earth. It is his *humanity* rather than his divinity that carries evolutionary empowerment. Second, he embodies a relational (some might prefer Trinitarian) mode of personhood very different from the Aristotelian notion of the robust patriarchal individual.

In the evolutionary context of the agricultural revolution, Jesus delivers an *affirmation, confirmation,* and *celebration* of all we humans had achieved in our long evolutionary journey of *seven million* years. Contrary to the story of conventional Christianity, Jesus did not come to rescue us from anything, because, for most of our evolutionary time, we got it right. Appearing at this historical (evolutionary) moment as the Christ-gestalt,[4] Jesus undoubtedly also serves as a pointer to our evolutionary future, exemplified perhaps in the extrasensory capacities often associated with the Risen Jesus. In a word, Jesus affirms our

Jesus affirms our past and opens for us new evolutionary portals toward which we are now unfolding.

past and opens for us new evolutionary portals toward which we are now unfolding.

Undoubtedly, many of these ideas will sound far-fetched, even bizarre to the contemporary reader. We have been so indoctrinated in the imperial way of being—fixated on stasis and time restriction, disconnected from creation, controlled by patriarchal power (requiring human subservience), dualistically split, and deprived of a grand narrative (briefly outlined in Genesis 1). We only know one meaningful narrative—of life and of faith—and that story has now become perverted and totally unsustainable. For our time, we need a new Christian myth, one that will be relevant and empowering for the twenty-first century.

THE MYTH REDISCOVERED

THEOLOGIANS AND SCRIPTURE scholars today frequently allude to *reworking the tradition*. Often the problem is that they don't go deep enough to recapture foundational truth. Science also advocates this strategy in a process known as *recapitulation*, the biogenetic law historically associated with Ernst Haeckel (1834–1919). In evolutionary terms, it highlights the fact that species at the embryonic stage often pass through the developmental stages of adult members of their species. Recapitulation may also be described as the long-jump syndrome. We step back several stages from the jump-off point in order to gather momentum to leap forward several steps. Metaphorically, we are drawing energy from the deep past in order to engage more creatively with the future.

In the Jesus story, the central myth seems to be that of *the Kingdom of God*, a topic extensively studied throughout the twentieth century but frequently retaining the patriarchal language. Archetypally, the notion of the kingdom of god has nothing to do with kings and imperial kingship. To the contrary, it embodies a total denunciation and rejection of the imperial understanding of God, so widely adopted by all formal religions. Instead, it denotes an anti-imperial stance of empowering mutual collaboration, with empowerment rather than power-over as the central feature.

To capture this new sense of the term Kingdom of God, I adopt a translation based more on Aramaic (the language spoken by the historical Jesus) rather than on biblical Greek, namely: *the Companionship of Empowerment.*[5] As Richard Rohr notes in his contribution to this edition of *Oneing*, this seems to have been the understanding that prevailed before Constantine adopted Christianity as the formal religion for the Roman Empire, setting new imperial foundations that have prevailed almost to the present time.

HAS CHRISTIANITY A FUTURE?

CURRENTLY, CHRISTIANITY is undergoing a huge evolutionary shift, marking the decline—and eventual death—of the imperial paradigm. What the new paradigm will look like is far from clear, but the following features are already illuminating the chaotic landscape:

- Christianity is likely to outgrow formal religion and become much more an earth-centred spirituality.[6]

- Reconfiguring the Jesus story within a Trinitarian relational web is one favoured reconstruction adopted by contemporary theologians.[7]

- The central focus on Jesus is likely to give way to the primacy of the Holy Spirit. Evidence for this may include two divergent movements of our time, (1) the recovery of the Great Spirit from indigenous spiritualities and (2) the spread of Pentecostalism.[8]

- The emerging Christianity will veer away from formal church structures and is likely to be grounded more in ecclesial networks, e.g., basic ecclesial communities.

- It will shed its long affiliation with power from the top down and flourish anew in wisdom from the ground up.

- Theologically, it will honor in a much more explicit way the guideline of Matthew 6:33: "Seek *first* the New Reign of God" (emphasis mine). The wisdom of the parables is likely to become a richer source for theological discernment.

- It will become a world-loving spirituality rather than an earth-denying religion, in which justice-making and ecological sustainability will be key qualities.

- Discerning the wisdom of Scripture and theology will become a lay prerogative with clerics fading into the background. A servant priesthood may return, but at this moment it is impossible to figure out how it might function.

FORWARD WE MOVE

What then surely is most new about our modern understanding of life is the idea of evolution, for it enables us to see life not as an eternally repeating cycle, but as a process that continually generates and discovers novelty.
—Lee Smolin

ACCORDING TO THE neo-DARWINIAN understanding, evolution moves forward in gradual segments, reworking the inherited models of the past and always looking to the past for guiding wisdom. Not so, our contemporary understanding of Growth —Change—Complexity. Here, the movement is more lateral than linear, contemplative rather than rational, open-ended rather than deterministic. It seeks to honor the past, but at the level of a deep story, not one engineered from the perspective of one or another power-filled ideology.

For Christians, Jesus still holds central inspiration, but more as a Spirit-filled person, and always reclaimed as the first disciple of the *Companionship of Empowerment* (the Kingdom). From within this context, all Christians—indeed, all humans—are invited to become adult co-disciples—"I do not call you servants, but friends" (John 15:15)—serving and earthing the Companionship of Empowerment.

Could any invitation be more luring, could any dream be more empowering? Let's pray for the grace that we will risk all and learn to flow with this evolutionary thrust. •

Abide in Me:

The Church's Love Affair with Christ

By Archbishop John C. Wester

PREDICTING THE FUTURE has never been a strong suit of mine. Yet, when I was asked to write an article for this issue of *Oneing* in response to the question, "What will the Catholic Church look like in the future?" I readily acquiesced. I suppose part of the reason I agreed has to do with the sexual abuse crisis facing the Catholic Church today, along with the social wars and ideological infighting that are so prevalent. Given these realities, the question seems fair and reasonable and thus deserving of a response. Having complete faith in our Lord's promise to be with the Church to the end of the age, I have no fear that predicting what the Church will look like down the road is merely an exercise in futility.

Actually, if we truly understand the Church today, we will have a pretty good picture of what it will be tomorrow. More than an institution, organization, or model (à la Cardinal Avery Dulles [1918–2008]), the Church is the fruit of love. The Church is, at its core, a body of believers who are drawn by the love of Christ to become the body of Christ through Baptism and the Eucharist. The Church is about relationships, just as God is about relationships: Father, Son, and Holy Spirit. The Church is about love, just as God is love. This is a Church of presence, of incarnation, and of "being there."

The theme of "presence" has become very significant for me, especially during this past season of Confirmation. I have been struck by the simple act of each candidate presenting oneself before the Church. In the sacrament of Confirmation, young women and men commit themselves to a future that they do not yet fully understand. It is a commitment which is born of promise and hope. They do not know what awaits them, what history holds, or what challenges must be faced, and what trials and persecution may be theirs. This is also true when we think of the Church of the future. We do not know what awaits us, what history will hold, which challenges must be faced, or what trials and persecutions may be ours.

So, when I reflect upon the future of the Church, it is born out of the simple act of presence. It is a true and real presence of Christ, in both the Eucharist and in the Body of Christ, the Church. I have come to realize that the Church of the future will only find its deepest meaning if it is born of this mystery of presence. To be present to another person, to a moment of history, to the wonder of God, requires us to step out of our selfish egos and into relationships. Relationship is the very mystery of God, for Christ has shown us that the essence of God, the very nature of God is to be in relationship. Creation, the Incarnation, the Mystery of the Church, and the ultimate destiny that awaits us all—each reveals and discloses the divine presence, relating to all.

All of this is nothing new. The Church has always been the fruit of a love affair with Christ. The primitive Church was no different. As my dear friend and mentor Archbishop John R. Quinn (1929–2017) wisely observed, if we are to understand the Church of the future, we must learn from the primitive Church. When the early Christians encountered the novel work of Paul, reaching out to the Gentiles, it created a crisis. According to Quinn, "This crisis of the primitive Church stands as a perpetual warning to the Church of every age that it cannot expect to find easy or quick solutions to its doctrinal and pastoral problems any more than the primitive Church did. Authentic discernment calls for evangelical patience, for openness to do the will of God, and for humble listening for the voice of God."[1]

If we wish to imagine the Church of the future, we need to dis-cover the mystery of the early Church hidden beneath the layers of history and legend. We must discover the abiding presence of Christ and the relational mystery of the Trinity. In other words, when I reflect upon the Church of the future, I am convinced that, regardless of its structure and organization, it will always have the "look of love"—not the romantic look made popular by the Burt Bacharach and Hal David song of 1967, but the look of love on the cross that gave birth to the Church as water and blood flowed from the side of Christ. This is the love that exists in relationships, in being present to God and to one another. It is this love that threads its way through the four indelible marks that characterize the Church, from its primitive beginnings to the present day and into the future. These are the marks that make the Church one, holy, catholic, and apostolic.

THE CHURCH AS ONE

THE CHURCH IS ONE because Christ is always at the center. Christ came to gather us together, to break down the walls that divide us, and to restore unity. Love unites, sin divides. The thrust of the incarnation and the Paschal mystery is a great universal miracle of ingathering. We know from the evangelist John, who allows us to eavesdrop on the intimate prayer of Jesus, that this wish for unity is Christ's most fervent prayer: "That they may all be one, just as you, Father, are in me, and I in you, that they also may be in us, so that the world may believe that you have sent me" (John 17:21). Thus, the Church is always about the business of "making one." The name of this publication suggests this same phenomenon. As Archbishop Quinn stated,

> The Church, as we see it in the pages of the New Testament, had a clear consciousness that it was a communion. It was not a group of isolated, independent communities. Nor has there been any evidence that the original communities were first indepen-dent groups, which later federated into a single Church. Instead, specific bonds joined these multiple communities into one Church from the beginning. At the level of doctrine, for instance, there was the fundamental conviction that all the Churches had

to be faithful to the original witness and teaching of the apostles as indicated in Acts: "They devoted themselves to the apostles' teaching..." (2:42). This meant that they held fast to the teaching with persistent tenacity. And because all the churches belonged to one Lord, embraced one faith, and were brought into being by one baptism, their members were brothers and sisters to one another. Consequently, at the level of service, they had some responsibility for one another. They expressed this by helping the poor in other churches and by offering hospitality to visitors and travelers from other churches.[2]

This unity with Christ leads to another bond and that is unity within the Church. Love of Christ inevitably leads to love of neighbor. Jesus forcefully and conclusively linked love of God and neighbor. Because the Church is the body of Christ, we see this linkage made manifest in the very person of Jesus. Reginald H. Fuller (1915–2007) and Daniel Westberg (1949–2017) put it beautifully: "There can be no love of God that does not express itself in love of neighbor. Conversely, there is no authentic love of neighbor that does not spring from love of God, for otherwise it is a refined, subtle form of self-love."[3]

This unity does not come easily. The divisions in our Church today speak clearly to this fact. Unity is not simply frosting on the cake, but is at the core of the Christian message. St. John of the Cross (1542–1591) got at this difficult reality in his first book of *The Ascent of Mount Carmel*. He wrote, as related by Iain Matthew, that we must "choose the person of Christ, and get used to making him, not [our]

The Church
of the future will only find
its deepest meaning if it is born
of this mystery of
presence.

feelings, [our] ultimate basis for action."[4] In other words, we have to lay aside our agendas, our egos, and our need for attention and allow Christ to draw us together. That is the universal mission of Christ in the Church. As St. John of the Cross wrote in *The Ascent*, we must "enter in utter nakedness, and emptiness, and poverty, for Christ."[5] This is the difficult stuff of relationships and unity.

THE CHURCH AS HOLY

THE CHURCH IS HOLY because Christ is holy, and Christ is at the heart of the Church. On most of my emails, I include a quote from Jean-Pierre de Caussade (1675–1751) which I believe says it all: "Faith sees that Jesus Christ lives in everything and works through all history to the end of time, that every fraction of a second, every atom of matter, contains a fragment of his hidden life and his secret activity."[6] The Church is holy, we are holy, because we are the branches on the vine. My Episcopal motto, "Abide in Christ," based on John 15:4, can be amplified by saying, "be holy as I am holy."

Unfortunately, many today confuse holiness with perfection. We, the Body of Christ, the Church, are holy because we are rooted in Christ, not because we have achieved nirvana. We are sinners and we need to be pruned and chastened and loved ever more, so that we can become holier as Christ is holy. St. Paul puts it beautifully when he says, "Even now, I have been crucified with Christ and the life I live now is not my own. Christ is living in me. I still live my human life, but it is a life of faith in the son of God who loved me and gave himself for me" (Galatians 2:19b–20). The Church is divine and human. In Christ, she will always be holy, but, in her humanness, she will always be in need of Christ's redeeming mercy and love.

I remember when, as a young auxiliary bishop in San Francisco, I was introduced by one of the priests, who said, "This is our new auxiliary bishop. It's the best we could do." I like to think he said that with tongue in cheek, but, in any case, he was quite right. Sin and imperfection are always part of who we are, but that does not mean that we cannot be holy. Being holy comes from Christ, abiding in Christ, and being nurtured by Christ. The Church, though imperfect, is holy because she, we, are caught up in Christ's love.

THE CHURCH AS CATHOLIC

James Joyce once said, in describing the Catholic Church, "Here comes everybody."[7] In keeping with the theme of love, this mark of the Church might be described as, "The Church is in love with everybody." This mark of the Church might be described as a gloss on the first mark, the Church is one. By that, I mean that the Church is not simply one with those that think alike and look alike and act alike. Rather, the Church is comprised of everyone. All are welcome. As my first pastor said in San Rafael, California, the Church doors are open to everyone. We do not have a Keep Out sign in the front. The Church is very much like a large projector which projects the face of Christ to the world. To the extent that there are people missing, Christ's face is incomplete. To the extent that the Church persecutes and abuses, the face of Christ is marred. The catholicity of the Church is rooted in its diversity. It is, I suppose, a human trait to circle the wagons, to be defensive and to engage in self-preservation. We tend to be suspicious of those who are different from us and yet Christ made it clear that the reign of God belongs to everyone. The Church, commissioned to gather all people into that reign, casts a wide net that excludes no one. It is our universal call.

I remember hearing a story from Sr. Marilyn Lacey, who worked with immigrants and refugees in the San Francisco Bay Area. She once picked up a refugee who had endured a long and grueling trip from her home country. Sister correctly guessed that she was quite hungry and prepared a meal for her. However, the newcomer did not touch her food. When Sister asked why the woman wasn't eating, she replied, "Where are the others?" Sister told her she didn't understand. The woman replied, "In my country, one would never eat alone. We always eat with the community." This sounds very much like the Eucharist to me. We are always missioned to go forth and gather people into our communion. Erasmo Leiva Merikakis has a wonderful reflection in which he paints a verbal picture of the Word of God acting like a tent that protects and guards us pilgrim believers. He then quickly adds that the pilgrim is not satisfied with simply being protected. Rather, he or she must consume the word, the protective covering, and go out to proclaim the good news. This is what it means to be Catholic and this will always be a mark of the Church.

Church relationships are radically inclusive, and the call to be relational will always include everyone. This is something to consider when celebrating the Eucharist together. When we get to the sign of peace, we are not simply flashing a Winston Churchill salute to our neighbor or wishing someone a pleasant day. Rather, as we prepare to go forward to receive the Body and Blood of Christ, made possible through his death and resurrection, the sign of peace is meant as an opportunity to say to the person to our right or left, regardless of who she or he is, "Just as Christ has died for me, so would I die for you, my brother, my sister." This takes "Catholic" to a new dimension.

THE CHURCH AS APOSTOLIC

To me, the previous three marks of the Church will always imply this fourth mark: the apostolicity of the Church. The Church is one in Christ, the Church is holy through Christ, and the Church is catholic because of Christ. As an apostolic Church, we are directly linked to Christ who came to proclaim the reign of God. The Church's mission, in turn, is to proclaim Christ. This commission came from Christ to the apostles. As was so eloquently stated in the Vatican II document *Lumen Gentium*,

> Christ is the Light of nations. Because this is so, this Sacred Synod gathered together in the Holy Spirit eagerly desires, by proclaiming the Gospel to every creature, to bring the light of Christ to all [people], a light brightly visible on the countenance of the Church. Since the Church is in Christ like a sacrament or as a sign and instrument both of a very closely knit union with God and of the unity of the whole human race, it desires now to unfold more fully to the faithful of the Church and to the whole world its own inner nature and universal mission.[8]

Being apostolic, the Church is even more than linked to the apostles. It also means that we enjoy the same apostolic intimacy with Christ through baptism. In the beginning of John's Gospel, Jesus invites his followers to abide with him. At the end of the gospel, Jesus invites them to abide in him. The Church abides in Christ, and therefore the Church is apostolic. To dwell in the heart of Christ is to dwell

The Church, organized religion, the communion of believers, whatever you wish to call it, is a communion of love.

or abide in the heart of the Father because that is Jesus' abode. This gets us right back to oneness and holiness, and to catholicity.

Being apostolic also implies that we, the Church, mediate Christ's grace to the world. Just as Christ had the apostles distribute the loaves and fishes to the multitude, so does he continue to commission us to be instruments of his nourishing grace. An apostolic Church is one that hears the cry of the poor and, like the apostles, gives her life for the many. This theme is certainly underscored in the ministry of Pope Francis. Having been nourished at the table of the Lord, we are called to go forth and to bring Christ to those we meet in our day-to-day lives. The images of field hospitals and the smell of the sheep are more than clever marketing ploys for Francis. Rather, they speak to the heart of Francis, who is doing all he can to break through the culture of indifference and keep the Church closely connected to Christ through his Petrine ministry.

To be one, holy, catholic, and apostolic is to be in love with Christ and those who make up his Body, the Church. As Jean-Pierre de Caussade wrote: "The whole business of self-abandonment is only the business of loving, and love achieves everything."[9] The Catholic Church has a very bright future as long as it stays in love with Christ. David Michael Stanley, SJ (1914–1996) once gave Mark's gospel the title, "How I Fell in Love with Jesus Christ." That is the mission of the Church, throughout the ages and into the future: to continually fall in love with Jesus Christ. The Church, organized religion, the communion of believers, whatever you wish to call it, is a communion of love. A God who is love could have no less.

To conclude, all of these themes come together for me as I recall an incident in my life many years ago. On a particularly (if not rare) sunny and quiet afternoon in San Francisco, I was making a visit to the Blessed Sacrament chapel at St. Thomas the Apostle parish. In the midst of my prayer, I was conscious that our Lord was not the only one present with me. I turned and saw a homeless man, whom we affectionately called Carnation Charlie (due to the flower he always wore in his lapel), staring at me. I said to him, somewhat brusquely, "Can't you see that I'm praying, Charlie?" He apologized and left. As I went back to my prayers, I had the sinking feeling that the "other presence" was not too happy with me. I ran outside and apologized to Charlie and was able to respond, finally, to his needs. It occurred to me that Charlie was not interrupting my visit with Christ, but that I was interrupting Christ's visit with me. Charlie was the one who was at home, abiding in the heart of Christ, and he was letting me in.

I suppose that sums up what religion is all about, what prayer is all about, and what presence is all about. It is all relational; it is all love. In the end, the Church will always have the look of love because that is the look on the face of Christ. Every fraction of a second and every atom of matter contains a fragment of his hidden life and his secret activity. As St. John of the Cross puts it in his poem "The Living Flame of Love,"

> Ah! gentle and so loving
> you wake within me, proving
> that you are there in secret and alone;
> your fragrant breathing stills me,
> your grace, your glory fills me,
> so tenderly your love becomes my own.[10]

Powering Down:
The Future of Institutions

By Richard Rohr

I N March of this year, I was visited by Dr. Max Watson, a
dear friend from Ireland, who is a worldwide expert in palliative
care. He is part of the faculty of Project ECHO, led by another
dear friend from East India, Dr. Sanjeev Aurora. They were having
their annual international teaching conference here in Albuquerque, at
their home base. Their work gives me great hope. So that you know
exactly where I am heading with this, I quote their vision and mission
statement directly and completely:

> Project ECHO is a lifelong learning and guided practice
> model that revolutionizes medical education and exponentially
> increases workforce capacity to provide best-practice specialty
> care and reduce health disparities. The heart of the ECHO
> model™ is its hub-and-spoke knowledge-sharing networks,
> led by expert teams who use multi-point videoconferencing

to conduct virtual clinics with community providers. In this way, primary care doctors, nurses, and other clinicians learn to provide excellent specialty care to patients in their own [local and often poor] communities.[1]

If, as is predicted, the world is heading toward a population of eleven billion people (we are now at six billion), the survival of the human species in any meaningful way is going to demand a radical revisioning and restructuring of all major institutions—in the very direction that ECHO is now proposing for healthcare. Our common life, if it is to be life at all, will surely depend on it.

Yes, we will always need highly educated specialists in all areas. However, they must all see their primary job as being the development of *multipliers* who are trained to use formats that are *highly accessible* to people in all parts of the world and at all levels of social class. Expertise has been hoarded for too long.

We thought the Internet was going to globalize us and, yes, it partly has. But we now realize it has also separated us into *enclaves of like-minded sources, untested by any mature community, that deeply reinforce our already-existing attitudes*—both for good and for ill. Right now, it scares many of us to think it might be mostly for ill: Hate congeals and gathers more hate, fear accumulates and creates more fear, whereas love does not automatically create more love. Love is often written off as softness or naïveté. Hatred is hard and certain. This all points to what Paulo Freire (1921–1997) called "circles of certainty,"[2] which need no basis whatsoever for their absolute certitude except their desire for private ego reinforcement.

At the same time, we are experiencing a very real temptation, worldwide, to move against our own democratic/equalizing ideals in favor of strongmen who can enforce, by some form of power, these same false certitudes. How can Donald Trump, Kim Jong-un, Rodrigo Duterte, Vladimir Putin, Jair Bolsonaro, Nicolás Maduro, and Xi Jin-

Expertise has been hoarded for too long.

ping all emerge in this short period of history—and after several centuries of what we thought was the gracious spread of democracy? How could this happen?

A TOP-DOWN WORLD

IT SEEMS THAT most civilizations, up to now, have looked to the "top" to save them. This is almost universally true. We actually do not mind kings, dictators, tyrants, and strongmen if they offer and promise what our particular circle of certainty wants. They have the power we envy and desire. They really seem to be our "saviors," particularly if we don't know what we really need. And, quite unfortunately, followers of Jesus, *who should have known better*, did not model or teach anything much different.

Jesus' most simple model of church was described as "wherever two or three are gathered in my name" (Matthew 18:20). Yet even this simple but clear promise of Divine Presence, "I am there in their midst," did not really make much of an impression on us! We Catholics like *bread presence* more than people presence, and the Protestants like *book presence* more than people presence. We all preferred some form of top-down authority: either a Pope (preferably infallible), a Patriarch in golden robes, an ordained and authoritative pastor, or a fully inerrant Bible in an otherwise totally errant world (interpreted by an inerrant teacher). Otherwise, we simply could not find our way to trust and enjoy the always available and ubiquitous Presence of God. This just cannot be true or ninety-nine percent of humanity will never know God's holiness and goodness—especially after all of creation and the whole universe seems to be saying that *God is anything but stingy!*

After the church aligned with the Western Roman Empire, beginning in 313, we have had a largely top-down version of the Gospel offered to us, which continues to this day. Then, after the Latin and Greek churches divided in the Great Schism of 1054, we repeated the pattern a second time (hatred and fear all over again!). We in the West sought security and authority through the Pope in Rome, and our Eastern brothers and sisters continued the same imperial pattern under the Emperors of Constantinople and Byzantium. I would have done the same amidst so much barbarism. But if you think there is no

We all preferred some form of top-down authority.

lasting enmity between East and West, read the history of the Crusades and the sacking of Constantinople by Western Christians. To be honest, the Eastern churches have never forgiven us, to this day—with patterns now frozen in a thousand institutionalized attitudes, prejudices, and practices. Orthodox monks literally ran out of the room in Romania when I, a Roman Catholic, accompanied by women—which seemed to make it worse—entered the room.

Despite the many good and much-needed Christian reforms inaugurated by the Protestant Reformation in the sixteenth century, the reformers did not generally change this top-down approach. It was the only way we could think at that time. *Cujus regio, ejus religio* ("Whatever region, his religion") took numerous forms in almost every European country and its respective worldwide colonies. Then, *colonization itself* became an imperial and disastrous misuse of the Gospel of Jesus. This led to the easy justification of the cruel enslavement of millions of Africans by Christian empires originating in Portugal, Great Britain, France, Spain, and the Netherlands. Once we had gone so far as to justify a "slaveholder religion," we no longer inhabited the same universe as Jesus.[3] Our moral compass has locked at due South. Yet this American version, emerging from the Southern United States, is the version that has been exported to much of the rest of the world—as if it had anything to do with the first two thousand years of Christianity.

This is an ahistorical version of Christianity because *Imperial Christianity needs to be, in some way, ahistorical for us to believe it!* It cannot let us know that our version of Christianity would never have been recognized by pre-313 Christianity. It has no validation in the Councils of the Church or the early Patristic period; was never believed by the Latin or the Greek church; was never taught by any mystic, saint, or legitimate reformer; is typically justified by its own strange "proof text" from Scripture; and is *always, always about power.* It is seldom a teaching about forgiveness, inclusion, simplicity, mercy, love, compassion, or understanding. These never tend to become central or mandatory issues, even though they clearly were for Jesus.

But we don't tend to divide over such issues because, too often, we are not invested in such issues. The major issues in which we invest invariably lend themselves to some kind of either-or thinking, or what we call dualistic thinking. Nine times out of ten, they have to do with power or gender: Who are the truly ordained? What keeps someone in the club? What excludes someone? What are acceptable variations on church governance? Who speaks for God? Who "has" God in their lineage, their apostolic succession, or their tabernacle? (As if we could "have" God.) Beyond who is saved, what are the requirements for or the enforcers of our particular salvation theory?

The answers in this arena are always dualistic! There is seldom subtlety or nuance, even though we are always dealing with Ultimate and Forever Mystery and are called to "be compassionate as God is compassionate" (Luke 6:36). Then, for some reason, the moral issues about which we are always absolutely certain are the very things Jesus never once talked about—so they can hardly be foundational or central—such as birth control, abortion, homosexuality, who is "worthy" to receive communion, and on and on. All of which returns me to my initial point.

FLATTENING OUT THE TRUTH

TOP-DOWN RELIGION has pretty much spoiled the show, up to now. (This is not to say that we do not need trained experts, scholars, leaders, and teachers.) But, as the medical community is learning from Project ECHO, we need to make the truths of both medicine and Christianity much more accessible, available, localized, and pastoral. Most people do not need to have major knowledge of theology or Scripture (which few priests or ministers have had anyway). Why not flatten out the huge and unbiblical distinction between clergy and laity to begin with?[4]

As the Project ECHO doctors have learned, none of us need to be specialists in everything. However, they discovered that, in most parts of the world, there are one or two major diseases. So they trained the local people, who knew everything about that one disease (diabetes, for example, or sickle cell anemia, or a skin disease), how to treat it. Then, if need be, they could send those locals for further training, to develop a higher level of expertise. It is the hub-and-spoke

Either we see Christ in everyone, or we hardly see Christ in anyone.

knowledge-sharing networks of ECHO, and it could be replicated in faith communities.

While Christian churches do much good, we have one huge pastoral problem that is making Christianity largely ineffective, and largely decorative, if you will allow me to say so. Yes, we often lack a lot of solid orthodox theology (yes, I am obsessed with it)—yet we clearly need good and compassionate pastoral and healing practices *ten times more!*

It seems to me that we must begin to validate Paul's original teaching on "many gifts and many ministries" (1 Corinthians 12:4–11) that together "make a unity in the work of service" (Ephesians 4:12–13). We need Christian people who are trained in, validated for, and encouraged to make home and hospital visits; do hospice work and jail ministry; support immigrants and refugees; help with soup kitchens; counsel couples before, during, and after marriage; teach classes in parenting; offer ministries of emotional, sexual, and relational healing; help with financial counseling; build low-cost housing; take care of the elderly; run thrift centers—all of which put Christian people in immediate touch with other people and for which no ordination is needed. Ordination would probably even get in the way. Remember, healing was most of the work Jesus appeared to do. It is almost too obvious.

Why are we not fighting over these positions? Why are there not many seminaries for training in these ministries, rather than one ministry called priesthood? Well, there is not much power, visibility, financial compensation, or any basic ego satisfaction in such flatland services. We reward the top (which is not the same as the most gifted or most generous) much more than we reward the middle or the bottom, probably because the top is where most of us want to be.

My vision of any future church needs to be much flatter and much more inclusive. Either we see Christ in everyone, or we hardly see Christ in anyone. Either we are Christ to everyone, or we cannot be

Christ to anyone. Frankly, my future church is much less "churchy," surely less patriarchal, and more concerned with its *mission statement* than with endlessly reciting our heavenly vision and philosophy statement—The Nicene Creed—every Sunday. There seem to be very few actionable items in most Christians' lives beyond attending Sunday services, which largely creates a closed and self-validating system. Another circle of certainty.

Simply put, any notion of a future church must be a fully practical church that is concerned about *getting the job of love done*—*and done better and better* (sort of like a business does with its products). Centuries of overemphasis on art and architecture, songs, liturgy, and prescribed roles have their place, but their overemphasis has made us a very top-heavy and, as I said earlier, a decorative church that is largely, and constantly, concerned with its own in-house salvation.

Most people today, in fact, understand church to mean a building, rather than where "two or three gather in [Jesus'] name," where the Divine Presence is promised just as certainly as it is promised in the bread, in the Bible, in the Sacraments, or in any anointed leadership: "I am in your midst" (Matthew 18:20).

Such leadership, I think, implies people who can spot, affirm, train, support, finance, and validate gifts and leadership wherever they see them in actual practice (read multipliers instead of monarchs). Then we are not all striving toward the top, but striving toward supporting the supreme work of love flowing into the world. I would call this model Non-Imperial Christianity.   •

The Future of Faith as the Way of Salvation

By Diana Butler Bass

I N THE ORIGINAL *Star Trek* television series, there was a running joke. Captain Kirk would ask Dr. McCoy to do something well beyond his ken, and the ship's medical officer would reply, "I'm a doctor, not a bricklayer!"—or a mechanic, coalminer, physicist, engineer, or whatever impossible task Kirk had assigned to him.

When faced with the question, "What is the future of Christianity?" I am tempted to respond, "I'm an historian, not a soothsayer!" Because, honestly, who can know? I have been asked this question myriad times over the last two decades, and I'm always still surprised when the request comes. Like Dr. McCoy, I am far more comfortable with what I know of the past than with tackling the impracticable request of discerning the contours of what-has-yet-to-be.

Despite his protests, however, McCoy would always lean into the impossible request, employing familiar instruments and his skills in new ways, most often to surprising effect. Rising to such occasions was often the only path out of whatever galactic crisis in which the crew of the *Enterprise* found itself. Perhaps McCoy's protest was half-hearted—I always suspected that he knew when we step beyond the safe territory of expertise, we discover new creativity and strength. Whatever the case, he and Captain Kirk always wound up saving the universe.

That is the sort of question posed here: "What is the future of Christianity?" It is a query at a time of crisis and one with uncertain answers. How can we courageously face an unsure future for Christian faith? Can we rise to impossibly difficult circumstances—challenges well beyond our expertise—in an age of doubt, pluralism, and struggles in the church?

I have no easy answers to these questions, but, having been asked them so many times, I have learned that the question is an invitation to spiritual creativity. To imagine the future of faith opens us to hear the world differently, to awaken to what we do not know, and to discover the power of simple actions.

FIRST, *the future calls us to hear differently.*

FEW THINGS ARE AS IMPORTANT as the spiritual practice of discernment. Indeed, if we listen well, the question itself—"What is the future of Christianity?"—may not be what we should even be asking at the moment.

Tangier Island is in the Chesapeake Bay. Europeans permanently settled there before the American Revolutionary War, the island is significant for its waterman culture, and it is listed as a National Historic Site. At the center of the community's life is a Methodist church, dating back to the beginning of not only the island's settlement but also of American Methodism itself.

This church survived by doing simple things—preaching, tending to the life of the islanders, caring for the needy, engaging formative practices of faith, and marking life with Christian rituals. It is a good church. It has been so for many generations. As church goes these days, it is a successful small community, having done what it needs to do to last well into the future.

But there is a problem: The island is sinking. In the next three or so decades, Tangier will slip into the bay, taking everything to a watery grave, including the church.

On Tangier Island, the question—"What is the future of Christianity?"—is essentially incoherent. Other questions are far more significant: "What is the future of the Bay, of the planet? What is our future?"

As I have ruminated on Tangier Island, I realize that far too many religious leaders are asking the wrong question. The future of Christianity matters little if there are no human beings, whether we extinct ourselves through war or environmental disaster. We can fix our denominations, bring new members to church, write the best theologies ever—and none of it will matter one whit if we are all dead. The question—"What is the future of Christianity?"—must be held in relation to other questions. Right now, the most significant of those questions is: "*What is the future of humankind?*"

That is the existential question of our time. All other questions pale by comparison and distract us from hearing the voices of God, the earth, and other creatures with the kind of rigor and compassion necessary for the living of these particular days. To me, the question about the future of Christianity has become: "What must Christians do to serve all creation when the island itself is in danger of sinking?"

Through deep listening, we arrive at better questions.

SECOND, *imagining the future awakens us to the importance of what we do not know.*

WHEN ASKING QUESTIONS about the future, hubris is our enemy. We need to develop the capacity to live with mystery and hold lightly to our own plans and predictions—and we often learn this capacity through failure.

Ray Dalio, one of the fifty wealthiest people in the world, is a wildly successful investment manager and a philanthropist committed to both the environment and education. But he was not always so successful, and he believes that income inequality is a global emergency. In the 1980s, as a bright young man with a brilliant Wall Street career ahead, he predicted that the United States was about to enter a major depression. He pulled back investments and wound up losing his fortune, having to borrow $10,000 from his parents just to survive. From this experience, he learned the importance of humility, especially in regard to principles of truthfulness and transparency. He developed new patterns of work and relationships (including spirituality and meditation) that ultimately propelled his financial success and generosity.

Almost twenty years ago, I was on a panel with Phyllis Tickle (1934–2015) at a large Episcopal conference. A diocese had just elected a bishop who was an out gay man, and the denomination was racked with apocalyptic fears of schism and the end of Anglicanism. During her comments, Phyllis spoke to the question of Christianity's future, making the case for inclusion based on sociology and her understanding of emergence. When she had finished, I looked at the audience and said, "I don't understand. For people who claim to believe in resurrection, we seem unduly afraid of death." Phyllis laughed, "Damn girl, that's the truth!"

Of course, I did not answer the questions worrying those at the conference. I only pointed out a mystery related to the inquiry. We believe in life after death. Somehow, in our enthusiasm to understand the trends and data, we had forgotten the mystery.

When it comes to the future of Christianity, so much is unknowable. Not only do we trust resurrection, but we also are at least dimly aware that time itself is a mystery. How can we talk about the future of Christianity when the God of the Bible is the One behind and beyond time? Do past, present, and future even exist for God? From a sacred perspective, everything that was still is; all that is continues to be; and that which will be is already. God holds all this within the divine presence—all time, from the fourteen billion years past when the universe broke forth until the moment when it will finally cease. If that isn't humbling, nothing is. We need to be deeply aware of these mysteries—resurrection and sacred time—when considering the future of anything, much less Christianity. When we trust what we do *not* know, when we live into things faith assures us are true, then humility empowers courage.

Right now, the most significant question is: *"What is the future of humankind?"*

THIRD, *we make the future when we act, especially when we bring our best selves to a crisis.*

BIG QUESTIONS like human survival and the mystery of time can be debilitating to people concerned about next year's steward-ship program or worrying if their grandchildren will be bap-tized. Life is an odd mixture of expansive vision and small actions, and it is in the space between the two that creative change often happens.

The model here is Jesus. Jesus knew all the big questions about the Reign of God and the humility of time. He preached about such things and welcomed his followers to experience both. But how can we live a generous and brave future? Mostly by telling stories, by feed-ing hungry people, by healing the suffering, and by drawing people into a new community based on love and gratitude. Jesus created a different future for humanity through radical small acts, by being the person he was and doing what he was called to do. In effect, Jesus showed up with his best self—his whole self—knowing what was at stake and living intentionally in relation to the Reign of God and the mystery he proclaimed.

We are often deluded by the idea that only big things can change the future. We feel overwhelmed by problems that demand impressive solutions, universal buy-ins, and large infusions of cash. We forget the power of simple acts of influence, of moments of compassion, of small stands for justice—how teachers, parents, friends, and even strangers can redirect the trajectory of history in a moment. If we truly believe that everything is connected, that we live in a sacred web, then every single action has influence over every other action. We are enormously powerful when we act to do what is good and beautiful and just—and in how we choose to react when something or someone threatens or shames us. When we bring our best, we might act out of expertise (as I might do as an historian or a writer), out of habit and practice (as in offering hospitality or praying), out of an emotional response (such as joy or surprise), or arising from a need (to protect a child or take care of someone injured). In reality, we all carry around a kind of life toolkit, sets of instruments and skills that can be employed at any time, but are especially helpful in case of emergency.

It never ceases to amaze me how often we deploy goodness. About a year ago, I was on a very long up-escalator out of the metro in Washington, DC. About ten steps above me was an older man

We are enormously powerful when we act to do what is good and beautiful and just.

who suddenly wobbled and then tumbled backward down the moving stairs, hitting his head several times. I stepped out of the way so as not to fall down the same stairs, but turned and ran after him, then squatted on the steps with him, all the while yelling for help and applying a scarf to stop the bleeding. Before I knew it, three young men had gathered around and, as the escalator arrived at street level, they carried him off. A woman was on her cell phone, calling 911. The man managed to tell us that friends were waiting for him in a local restaurant. Another stranger ran to find them. I sat praying with the man, who was in shock and bleeding from an open wound on his head.

All of this happened quickly—almost a dozen people, all strangers, formed a swarm of love to help someone they never met, and each brought something needed to the crisis. About twenty minutes later, an ambulance arrived and we all dispersed, not one of us even knowing the name of anyone else. I still think about the man, wondering about his friends, his spouse, his children—how he might have died without that helping brigade. I think of the others, too: What brought each to that moment, how every person contributed to a good outcome, and how strangers could move together to save a life. We changed his future that day; we most likely changed our own futures as well.

WHEN IT COMES to the future of Christianity, that's it: It is not what we think, it is far more than we can imagine, and we make it through our actions. I could quote trends, opine on the failures of church, teach about emergence, offer insights from organizational development, or write about panentheism and process theology, but the truth of the matter is much simpler: We bear a beautiful story—one about life and death and compassion and justice and the cosmos and God—with all its mystery and tenderness and wild unpredictability.

And we show up. We might show up with forethought and planning, or we might just show up when the crisis is underway. We do what is necessary in the moment, what we are asked to do, acting as one for the sake of love. In the process, like Kirk and McCoy, we might just save the universe—or, at the very least, open new possibilities for the Christ-way to lighten and enlighten humanity as turbulent waters rise around us. The future of Christianity is ultimately true salvation—*salvus*—to both rescue and heal all that God loves. •

Loving the
Church Back
to Life

By Shane Claiborne

C HRISTIANITY IN AMERICA is in a funk.
Catholics have the sexual abuse scandals. Methodists are
on the brink of splitting or collapsing over the LGBTQIA+
inclusion debate. Southern Baptists are experiencing a mass exodus, in
part because they continue to deny that women can be pastors. Some
of the reformed folks and Calvinists just issued a statement that social
justice has nothing to do with the Gospel. And 81 percent of white
evangelicals voted for Trump. That's my tribe: The same people who
led me to Jesus have led us to Trump—and continue to defend him.

That's what I mean by a funk.

AMERICAN CHRISTIANITY TODAY

WITHOUT A DOUBT, one of the biggest obstacles to Christ is Christians. We talk about grace, but we support the death penalty at a higher rate than the general population. We worship a Savior who said, "Love your enemies" (Matthew 5:44), but we are the biggest supporters of military spending. We preach about Jesus saying, "Turn the other cheek" (Matthew 5:39), but Christians are "standing our ground" as the highest gun-owning demographic in America.

It's been said that Trump did not change America—he *revealed* America. It's also fair to say that Trump didn't change American Christianity, he just revealed it.

What we see is very disturbing. It's understandable why many people, especially young people, are leaving the church—but I'm hopeful, nonetheless.

Many people say that they are done with the church, but they are really done with Trump, and with Trump-evangelicalism. Others say that they are done with Christianity, but they've really just rejected a version of American nationalism that camouflages itself as Christianity, but doesn't look like Christ at all.

The danger is inoculation. When you get a watered-down version of a virus, it knocks the virus out of your system, and there are many people in the US who, I fear, are being inoculated by a watered-down version of Christianity.

So, what is the best way forward?

CHRISTIANITY IN CONTEXT

THERE WAS A TIME, in the 1980s and 90s, when the response to the hypocrisies in the church was to start new, creative expressions of church—what many came to call "the emerging church movement." My community in Philly, The Simple Way, was one of the fruits of that era, even though we've never had a traditional Sunday morning service.

Now, things are a little different. Many of the reactionary movements today are less constructive and generative than two decades ago, and promote leaving the institutional church altogether—trends like #ExEvangelicals and #EmptyThePews are regular on Twitter. They want Jesus, but not the church. They want to be spiritual, but not religious. They want to be mystics, but aren't very interested in the spiritual practices that that gave birth to the mystics of old.

Much of this energy is coming from post-evangelicals, recovering fundamentalists, and disenchanted Catholics. It is a movement of deconstruction. Some conferences can feel like post-evangelical, ex-Catholic group therapy.

The problem is that many people are deconstructing things that this generation has not even begun to construct—and that is also why I'm hopeful. Many new movements have been born amid the remnants of the past. Fresh life can come from the compost of Christendom. I think we are poised for another great awakening.

But we must channel discontentment with the way things are into constructive renewal. Just like the phrase popularly attributed to Mahatma Gandhi, "Be the change you want to see in the world," we need to be the change we want to see in the church.

Saying that we can be Christians without the church is sort of like someone who had an abusive mother saying the solution to bad mothers is to have no mothers. The problem is, you can't have children without mothers, and you can't have Christians without a church.

Only a person with a mother can say we don't need mothers. A generation that no longer believes in mothers will have a hard time giving birth to anything.

St. Cyprian (c. 200–258) said, "You cannot have God for your Father if you don't have the Church for your Mother."[1] Now, I don't think that means we have to leave a dysfunctional mother the way she is. In fact, just the opposite: We need to love her and help her recover, perhaps protect ourselves in cases of abuse, but never give up on her—because God specializes in redemption.

God is restoring all things. Institutions like the church are broken, just like people, and they too are being healed and redeemed. My friend Chris Haw put it this way. It's the difference between being in

I think we are poised for another great awakening.

a canoe and a rowboat. In a canoe, you look forward as you row, but in a rowboat, you look back as you move forward. Our way forward is behind us.

I also heard Chris, whom I consider one of the sharpest young Catholic theologians in the US, describe why he is joining the Catholic Church at a time when many folks are leaving the Catholic Church. He said it is the same reason he moved into Camden, New Jersey, which, at the time he moved there, was rated the worst place to live in America. In short, he believes in resurrection and that God is redeeming all things—including Camden and the church.

I don't believe anything is born outside the ecclesial family tree. Certainly, I'm not proud of everything in the church's family tree. Neither am I proud of everything in my own family history, but we own it, and we continue to build the kind of family we know God wants.

Twenty years ago, when folks asked me if I was Protestant or Catholic, I would say, "No." I would go on to explain that I was a follower of Jesus and Jesus was not to be confined by sectarianism. Now, when folks ask me if I am Protestant or Catholic, my answer is slightly different. I say, "Yes," and I mean it. I have been shaped by both traditions, and I need the whole family tree of the Church, with a big C. Rather than throw out the traditions, I want to know and study them, find the treasures and spit out the bones.

The church needs discontentment. It is a gift to the Reign of God, but we have to use our discontentment to engage rather than to disengage. We need to be a part of repairing what's broken rather than jumping ship. One of the pastors in my neighborhood said, "I like to think about the church like Noah's Ark. That old boat must have stunk bad inside, but if you tried to get out, you'd drown."

Let's live like Jesus really meant the stuff he said.

RECLAIMING CHRISTIANITY

J UST AS WE CRITIQUE the worst of the church, we should also celebrate her at her best. We need to mine the fields of church history
and find the treasures, the gems. We need to celebrate the best that
each tradition can bring—I want the fire of the Pentecostals, the
love of Scripture of the Lutherans, the political imagination of the
Anabaptists, the roots of the Orthodox, the mystery of the Catholics,
and the zeal of the evangelicals.

One of the most promising things that has come out of the emerging church has been folks looking back and reclaiming the best of their
traditions, seeing that it's not an either/or but a both/and—God is
doing something ancient and something new. Phyllis Tickle called
it "hyphenated denominations"—Presby-mergence, Bapti-mergence,
Luther-mergence—because what they are doing is renewing and
building on what was.

Many of the Salvation Army folks and Mennonites are looking
back as they move forward. They are remembering the best of their
traditions, which have kept alive the peace tradition of the faith. Their
simple living, deep community, and restorative justice are just as relevant today as they were a few hundred years ago. We need a new
Anabaptist renewal to help us combat the myths of our culture—that
happiness must be purchased or that war can bring peace. The Mennonites were some of the best countercultural Christians in history.
They went to jail and got killed for their uncompromising faith. We
need that kind of courage in this age of Trump.

A couple of years ago, the world lost Phyllis Tickle, a wonderful
woman and very influential Christian leader and writer. She often
mentioned that the church needs a rummage sale every few hundred
years. We have to get rid of the clutter, discover forgotten treasures,
and dust off the family heirlooms. Last year marked the five hundredth
anniversary of the Reformation, which was one of the most significant
moments in the history of Christianity. The reformers were navigat-
ing many of the same currents and contradictions that we are trying
to navigate today. Perhaps it's time for another rummage sale, a new
reformation.

If we are going to survive this current crisis, I want to offer a few
suggestions as we think toward the future.

FIX OUR EYES ON JESUS

IRST, LET US fix our eyes on Jesus. When we lose Christ as the "cornerstone," everything else is on shaky ground. The best antidote for toxic evangelicalism is actually Jesus. Our brother Rev. William Barber, who has been a prophetic voice since the last presidential election season, says "Christian [nationalists] 'say so much about areas where the Bible says very little'—abortion, homosexuality—'and speak so little about the issues where the Bible says so much,' like poverty, empathy, and justice."[2]

That's what gave birth to the movement we call Red Letter Christians, which is now international—a big tent for organizing and movement work, connecting Christians who love Jesus and justice.

It all started with a radio host in Nashville, Tennessee. He was interviewing a friend of ours, Jim Wallis, and the host didn't seem to have too much to do with Christianity. He mentioned having read most of the Bible. There were parts he really liked, and other parts he found confusing, but then he said something interesting. Referring to the old Bibles which have the words of Jesus highlighted in red, he said, "I've always liked the stuff in red. You all seem to like the stuff in red. You should call yourselves Red Letter Christians." And it stuck.

Here's our covenant at Red Letter Christians:[3]

> I dedicate my life to Jesus, and commit to live as if Jesus meant the things he said in the "red letters" of Scripture.

> I will allow Jesus and his teaching to shape my decisions and priorities.

> I denounce belief-only Christianity and refuse to allow my faith to be a ticket into heaven and an excuse to ignore the suffering world around me.

> I will seek first the Kingdom of God—on earth as it is in heaven—and live in a way that moves the world towards God's dream, where the first are last and the last are first, where the poor are blessed and the peacemakers are the children of God,

working towards a society where all are treated equally and resources shared equitably.

I recognize that I will fall short in my attempts to follow Jesus, and I trust in God's grace and the community to catch me when I do.

I know that I cannot do this alone, so I commit to share this journey with others who are walking in the way of Jesus. I will surround myself with people who remind me of Jesus, help me become more like him and hold me accountable for my actions and words.

I will share Jesus with the world, with my words and with my deeds. Like Jesus, I will interrupt injustice, and stand up for the life and dignity of all. I will allow my life to point towards Christ, everywhere I go.

Let's live like Jesus really meant the stuff he said. Let's imagine a Christianity that looks like Jesus again, a faith worth believing, an evangelicalism that is known for love again. Let's stop complaining about the church that we've experienced and build the church of which we dream.

Jesus must be the foundation for all our political convictions. He is the lens through which we understand the world, and the Bible. There's an old hymn that goes like this,

My hope is built on nothing less
than Jesus' blood and righteousness....
On Christ the solid rock I stand,
all other ground is sinking sand.[4]

The answer is not less Jesus, but more Jesus.

Over the centuries, Christians, at their best, have refused to place their hope in anything short of Jesus. After all, the word "vote" shares the same root as "devotion" and has everything to do with where we rest our hope and where our loyalty lies. Our devotion to Jesus and the "least of these" creates the framework for how we think about every issue, whether it is immigration, capital punishment, abortion, or healthcare. The answer is not less Jesus, but more Jesus.

EMBRACE A CONSISTENT ETHIC OF LIFE

SECOND, LET'S BE champions of life.

In a world filled with violence, one of the most important things we can talk about today is the need for a consistent ethic of life. I like to say that I am pro-life from the womb to the tomb. Every human being is made in the image of God, and any time a life is lost we lose a little glimpse of God in the world. In order for evangelicalism to recover from the contradictions for which it has become famous, it will need a consistent life ethic. To be pro-life is not only about protecting the unborn, but also about supporting folks after they are born. This language of the consistent ethic of life, the seamless garment, has been a helpful ethical framework for many people over the centuries. The early Christians stood consistently against all killing, and have spoken passionately throughout history against abortion, the death penalty, murder, and war. Today, a consistent life ethic is resonating with a new generation of evangelicals, especially young folks.

All of us who seek to be pro-life should continue to care about abortion, but we should just as passionately care about the death penalty, gun violence, the movement for black lives, the crisis of refugees and immigrants, the environment, healthcare, mass incarceration, and all the other issues that are destroying the lives and squashing the dignity of children whom God created and loves so deeply.

DECENTER WHITENESS

THIRD, WE NEED to decenter whiteness. There is a giant fault line of race in America, and it is evident in the church as well, even in progressive circles. Consider the books you've read over the past year. How many of them were written by women of color and non-white voices?[5] Those of us who are white need to intentionally and more frequently put ourselves in places where we are a minority. A lot of our big visions for "racial justice" and "multiculturalism" begin small. Racial reconciliation begins in our homes, at our dinner tables, and in our living rooms. Consider joining a church or organization led by a person of color.

For those who are feeling like leaving the church, consider this. Leaving fundamentalism or toxic evangelicalism doesn't mean leaving the Christian faith. There is more to the church than white evangelicalism. If you are turned off by Trump-evangelicalism, that doesn't mean you have to leave the church. Consider joining a church led by a pastor who is not a part of the white evangelical establishment. In contrast to the 81 percent of white evangelicals who voted for Trump, 72 percent of evangelicals of color voted differently, and they are the fastest growing population of Christians, making up over a third of evangelical Christians in America. They love Jesus and they know that justice is a core part of the Christian faith.

FOCUS ON SPIRITUAL FORMATION AND DISCIPLESHIP

THE POLITICAL CRISIS is also a moral and spiritual crisis, and one of the antidotes is to put a renewed focus on spiritual formation and discipleship. For too long, evangelicalism has been defined by beliefs rather than practice, by doctrines rather than actions. When we focus on beliefs alone, we end up with great theologians, televangelists, and preachers. When we focus on lifestyle Christianity, we produce saints. That's what we need today—not just more preachers, but more saints.

We can maintain our orthodoxy ("right thinking") while reclaiming our orthopraxis ("right living"). There is some sloppy theology out there and we cannot let go of our core beliefs, such as the bodily resurrection. If our theology does not include the bodily resurrection, then it is not Christianity. But, we also must be people of orthopraxis. If our religion does not include welcoming immigrants and refugees, then it is not Christianity either. Our big challenge today is not just right thinking but right living—and the two must go together like the two blades of a pair of scissors.

The political crisis is also a moral and spiritual crisis, and one of the antidotes is to put a renewed focus on spiritual formation and discipleship.

Doctrinal statements are important, but they are hard to love. God did not just give us words on paper; the Word became flesh, and now we are to put flesh on our faith. In the end, Christianity spreads best, not by force, but by fascination. The last few decades of evangelicalism have become less and less fascinating. We've had much to say with our mouths, but, often, very little to show with our lives. People cannot hear what we say because our hypocrisies are too loud. It's time to sing a better song. That's why this current crisis is solved, at least in part, with better spiritual formation and discipleship.

Here's what I've come to realize with the recent emphasis on authenticity: People do not expect Christians to be perfect, but they do expect us to be honest. The problem is that, much of the time, we have not been honest. We've pretended to be perfect and pointed fingers at other people. Then, when we get caught doing the same things we have called out in others, we are doubly guilty. There really is something to this idea of "Judge not, that you not be judged" (Matthew 7:1, NKJV). When we preach about how wrong it is to smoke, and then we get caught smoking, people are naturally ticked. The question isn't whether or not we are hypocrites. The question is, are my own hypocrisies a little less today than they were yesterday?

I went to a church recently where the greeters had interesting attire. Instead of suits and ties, they wore t-shirts that said: "NO PER-FECT PEOPLE ALLOWED."

The good news is that Jesus didn't come for folks who have it all together, but for folks who are willing to admit they are falling apart (Matthew 9:13). It's not about how good we are, but how good God is. Hopefully, that can also give us some grace with a church full of messed-up people, and with ourselves. We are imperfect people, falling in love with a perfect God, and doing our best to become more like the One we worship.

The church is meant to be the moral conscience of society, to preach repentance and grace—and sometimes it feels like we've forgotten both in America. Too often, we have been the chaplains of the empire and defenders of the status quo rather than the prophetic conscience of the nation. We've often blessed the rich rather than the poor and stood by the warmakers instead of the peacemakers. We've defended the powerful rather than the weak and exchanged the cross for a gun.

Our current crisis is not just a theological one, and not just a political one. This is a love crisis. Our country is being held captive to fear, and fear is the enemy of love. Scripture promises, "Perfect love casts out fear" (1 John 4:18), and we can see from this current administration that fear also casts out love. When fear, rather than love, compels us, we do really terrible things to other people. This is a moment where we must decide which master we will serve—love or fear—and many have chosen fear.

Let us choose love—for they will know we are Christians by our love. •

Three Christianities

By Brian D. McLaren

C HRISTIANITY OF THE FUTURE will almost certainly be at
least two things. I hope and pray that it will be a third as well.
First, Christianity of the future will be people, congregations, and denominations doing exactly what they're doing now.
Whether they're *piano-and-stained-glass chapels-in-the-country*, or *rock-and-roll-big-screen-megachurches-in-the-suburbs*, or *big-steeple-and-pipe-organ-cathedrals-in-the-city*, they'll keep doing what they've been doing because
they're sincere traditionalists and that's what traditionalists do.

Sure, they'll make a concession here or there as times change, but
I don't doubt for a minute that a hundred years from now, there will
still be Christian communities doubling down on traditional doctrine,
hierarchy, liturgy, polity, and style.

If they're more conservative traditionalists, we can expect them
to continue keeping women "in their place" and LGBTQIA + people
in the closet (or out the door). We can expect them to recite the
same dogma, world without end, faithfully answering questions of
the fourth or seventeenth centuries while remaining oblivious to the

pressing questions of today. We can expect them to proclaim the same evacuation gospel (aka a "sin-management gospel") that seeks first and foremost to enter heaven after death rather than seeking first God's reign and justice here and now on earth. We can expect them to remain centered on buildings and budgets, pulpits and organs (or bands and lighting), and committees and bylaws (or brands and target markets).

This traditionalist sector will be sure to keep the buildings open, even though fewer and fewer people come; to keep the liturgy going, even though fewer and fewer people have much idea why; and to keep their pastors employed (often, barely), even though the purpose of their employment will be less and less clear. Their work won't be easy, but they will pour their hearts into it, sincerely, because "doing what we've always done" is all they've been taught to do.

"Doing what we've always done" will likely lead to continuing numerical decline by a few percentage points (or more) with each new generation, but I don't doubt this traditionalist sector will last a long, long time, doing much good along the way. (Among many reasons for its longevity, this form of Christianity has so much wealth that it can simply liquidate assets to keep serving a dwindling clientele and sustaining a professional clergy for a long, long, long time.)

Second, along with a traditionalist sector, Christianity of the future will almost certainly contain a regressive, authoritarian wing: hyper-patriarchal, anti-immigrant, xenophobic, homophobic, Islamo-phobic, nationalist, white supremacist, and militarist. We see this nos-talgic/regressive strain of Christianity growing right now in many places in the world.

Here in America, we see it in Catholics more devoted to the teach-ings of Steve Bannon, Bill O'Reilly, and Sean Hannity than Fr. Richard Rohr, Sr. Simone Campbell, or Sr. Joan Chittister (or even Pope Fran-cis). Similarly, we see a majority of Evangelicals and other Protestants proud to join Jerry Falwell, John Hagee, Franklin Graham, and Robert Jeffress as fervent followers of Donald Trump, resurrecting what many have called the old "slaveholder religion" of the American South.

Meanwhile, in Russia and elsewhere, we see regressive Orthodox Christians striking deals with Vladimir Putin and other authoritarian strongmen, trading political protection and favors for a willingness to remain silent about political corruption and violations of human rights (including religious freedom) for ethnic and religious minorities.

This new kind of Christianity can only emerge as a *trans-denominational movement of contemplative spiritual activism.*

This kind of racialized, regressive Christianity (some call it Christo-fascism) has proven very useful to dictators and demagogues through the centuries, not to mention their corporate associates. For that reason, it will probably gain strength in the coming turbulent years, attracting the anxious who find comfort in authoritarian leadership, while driving many, especially the young, away from any kind of Christianity (or organized religion) for good.

Obviously, these two Christianities, traditionalist and regressive, already overlap and, in some places, they will probably merge in the not-too-distant future. The open question is to what degree they will "ruin the brand" of Christianity before they are either reformed or destroy themselves (and perhaps civilization along with them).

That's why more and more of us are hoping, praying, and dedicating ourselves to a third form of Christianity. This new kind of Christianity can only emerge as a *trans-denominational movement of contemplative spiritual activism.*

Although the signs of its emergence are already visible in many places, we should remember that movements are fragile in their early stages, which means that this fledgling movement may be suppressed, set back, or squashed for years, decades, or longer by traditional and regressive sectors of the Christian community that see it as a threat. It also may make fatal errors that cause it to self-sabotage, if not self-destruct. Either way, a major collapse of one or both of the first two forms of Christianity may need to happen before the third comes into full fruition. (I hope that will not be necessary.)

This third possible Christian future has seized my imagination for decades now, and I've written thousands of pages about it. I'd like to mention just three characteristics of it that strike me as deeply important.

First, this emerging or emergence Christianity (as Fr. Richard Rohr and I have called it, along with Phyllis Tickle and many others) will be *decentralized and diverse* rather than centralized and uniform. In other words, it will have the shape of a movement rather than an institution. It will be drawn together, not by external uniformity of doctrine, hierarchy, polity, liturgy, or style, but by internal unity of way of life, mission, practices, and vision for the common good.

In his article "Powering Down," Fr. Richard makes a bold claim in this regard: On a small planet with an exploding human population, human institutions must go through a radical shift in paradigm. Instead of hoarding and centralizing resources like expertise, education, mentoring, and authority, we need to multiply them and democratize them.

This, of course, was Jesus' original approach. He never announced to his disciples: "Hey folks, we're going to start a new, centralized, institutional religion and name it after me." Instead, he played the role of a nonviolent leader and launched his movement with the classic words of movement, "Follow me" (see Matthew 4:19, for example). He used his power to empower others. He did great things to inspire his followers to do even greater things. Rather than demand uniformity, he reminded his disciples that he had "sheep of other folds" (John 10:16) and that "whoever is not against us is for us" (Luke 9:50). He recruited diverse disciples who learned—by heart—his core vision and way of life. Then he sent these disciples out as apostles to teach and multiply his vision and way of life among "all the nations" (Matthew 28:19).

As he repeatedly explained, the dangerous, turbulent, uncertain times, together with the failure of existing institutions, made this strategy essential: "The time is ripe," he said (Luke 10:2, slightly paraphrased), "and we need more laborers." (This pattern of multiplying leader/teacher/practitioners is exactly the pattern we find, not only with Jesus in the Gospels, but also with Paul throughout the New Testament, in places like 2 Timothy 2:2 and 1 Corinthians 11:1.)

· As in Jesus' day, so in ours. Each day, climate change and other ecological crises converge with an obscenely wide and fast-growing gap between the elite classes and the struggling masses. With each day, a global weapons industry converges with militarist national economies around the world to produce more and more weapons with more and more kill-power. In light of this death-dealing convergence, we need an alternative life-giving convergence capable of rapid adaptation and evolution, a vital new kind of Christianity that spreads a message of good news for the planet, for the poor, and for those who long for peace.

That's why, in dangerous times like these, we can't afford to produce nice, quiet, compliant Christians on the one hand, or angry, oppositional, fear-driven reactionaries on the other. Instead, we have to produce generations of dedicated, courageous, and creative contemplative activists who will join God to bring radical healing and change to this damaged world, before it's too late.

We need this movement—not someday, maybe, but right now, definitely.

That brings us to the second characteristic I'd like to name: The diverse and decentralized movement we need will be *radically collaborative*, working with, across, and, when necessary, outside of and in spite of existing institutions to seek the common good. It will not be *anti-institutional* because institutions are necessary for human survival, but neither will it be *institutional*, in the sense that it is preoccupied with its own survival or bringing benefits only to its members. Rather, it will be *trans-institutional*, working across institutions, both religious and non-religious, seeking the common good of those inside and outside the movement and the institutions it involves.

If we picture our existing denominational and institutional structures as a set of vertical silos, we could picture this movement mobilizing and aligning across the forward-leaning wing of all of the silos—not eradicating them, not competing with them, but, instead, coexisting with them and using their support wherever possible for mutual advantage (and, when necessary, ignoring their pretensions of sovereignty).

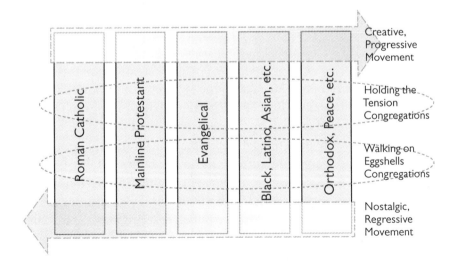

The fact is, this creative and progressive movement for a new kind of Christianity provides an alternative to three other stances present across institutional silos: (1) the well-organized and sometimes militant nostalgic/regressive movement of the religious right, (2) the "walking on eggshells" privatized religion that fears offending major donors and so always plays it safe, saying and doing little to nothing deemed controversial, and (3) the "holding the tension" churches that are caught in the middle, trying to find a way forward:

We could adapt the diagram slightly to acknowledge the reality and importance of other institutions within the Christian community, including religious orders, seminaries, colleges, organizations for children and youth, publishing, media, and other para-church ministries.

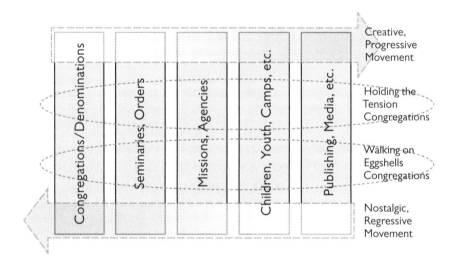

Across the religious landscape, the two centrist groupings comprise the traditionalist churches that are walking on eggshells and holding the tension created by the progressive and regressive wings moving in opposite directions. I doubt that the future will get easier for them, as two very different visions for the future of Christianity play out. The ruptures we see in some denominations represent in large part an inability or refusal for traditionalists to coexist with two such different movements. Some are pulled forward, others back. In this way, the word *division* accurately represents two divergent visions of what a Christian community is and should be.

The third and most important aspect of this third form of Christianity in the future is simple, obvious, and yet radical: it is about love, as Jesus taught and embodied.

Not long ago, someone quoted a statement that went something like this: "Our founder was focused on love but we have, instead, been focused on our founder. When will we realize that the best way to honor our founder is not to be about him, but, rather, to be about what he was about?" The statement reflects Jesus' own concern about those who say, "Lord! Lord!" but don't do what he taught (Matthew 7:21).

There's no question what Jesus was about. He didn't say, "By this will all people know you are my disciples: by your doctrinal purity." Nor did he say, "This is the first and greatest commandment: to carry out the liturgy faithfully every Sunday." Nor did he say, "This is my new commandment, that you sing lots of songs and say 'Praise Jesus!' a lot!" Nor do we find Paul writing, "Now, these three things remain: liturgy, polity, and inerrancy (papal or biblical), and the greatest of these is inerrancy."

No. The New Testament makes it abundantly clear that Jesus was about love first and foremost, in word and deed. Jesus began with love for God, but inseparably linked that love with love for neighbor, with the understanding that neighbor includes the other, the outsider, the outcast, the last, the least, the lost, the disgraced, the dispossessed, and the enemy. This love for neighbor was, in turn, inextricably related to an appropriate love for self. In fact, to love neighbor as oneself leads to the realization that oneself and one's neighbor are actually distinct yet inseparable realities. In today's world, we must add that, for Jesus, God's love extends to the wildflower, the meadow grass, the sparrow,

In this desirable future, every willing Christian congregation makes every competing interest subsidiary to love.

and the raven. He saw all of God's creatures as part of one heavenly realm, as did dear St. Francis, and as do more and more of us.

When I think of this third kind of Christianity of the future, then, I think of a movement of revolutionary love. I see it as distinctively Christian, but not in any exclusive way, because if we truly see love as Jesus' point and passion, then the depth of our devotion to Christ will always lead us to love our Jewish, Muslim, Hindu, Buddhist, Sikh, Indigenous, nonreligious, agnostic, atheist, and other neighbors *as ourselves.*

In fact, the robust pneumatology of this new kind of Christianity will send us into the world, expecting to see the Spirit of love at work everywhere: not just in our religion, but in other religions; and not just in religion in general, but in the arts, in business, in education, in agriculture, in government, in philosophy, in sport, in science, in homemaking, in family, and in every other dimension of human life. (In fact, we could easily put these labels on the silos in the diagrams above.)

Our job will be to decisively and continually surrender our lives as living sacrifices, to offer ourselves to be ongoing embodiments of the cosmic Christ, so we can play the little musical instrument of our bodies for our little time on the stage in this ever-expanding cosmic symphony of love.

In this desirable future, every willing Christian congregation makes every competing interest subsidiary to love, which is the fruit of all contemplation and the goal of all action. If we embody this third form of Christianity, if we make real this alternative Franciscan orthodoxy, if we become the seeds of a movement of contemplative activism in the Spirit of Christ, I can imagine hundreds of thousands of congregations, whether comprised of two or three, or two or three thousand, each a locally and globally engaged school of love, teaching future generations to discover, practice, and live in love: love for our neighbor, love for ourselves, love for all creatures and all creation—all comprising love for God, who is all in all in all.   •

The Prophetic Future of Christianity

By Nontombi Naomi Tutu

Then Amaziah, the priest of Bethel, sent to King Jeroboam of Israel, saying, "Amos has conspired against you in the very center of the house of Israel; the land is not able to bear all his words. For thus Amos has said,

'Jeroboam shall die by the sword,
and Israel must go into exile
away from his land.'"

And Amaziah said to Amos, "O seer, go, flee away to the land of Judah, earn your bread there, and prophesy there; but never again prophesy at Bethel, for it is the king's sanctuary, and it is a temple of the kingdom."

Then Amos answered Amaziah, "I am no prophet, nor a prophet's son; but I am a herdsman, and a dresser of sycamore trees, and the Lord took me from following the flock, and the Lord said to me, 'Go, prophesy to my people Israel.'"

—Amos 7:10–15

As someone raised in South Africa, I felt the Hebrew Bible prophets seemed to speak directly to our situation. Of those, Amos has always been one of my favorite prophets and this particular reading has been my favorite of favorites—it has become something of a touchstone for me. Strange as it might seem, this ancient text speaks to me of where the Christian Church is today and where it seems to be heading. Amos and Amaziah represent for me the two dominant models of the church today, and what Christianity looks like in the future will be decided by which model we, as a community of faith, decide to follow: Amaziah or Amos.

First, we have Amaziah, who is not ashamed to refer to the temple at Bethel as the "king's sanctuary and . . . a temple of the kingdom." How can God's temple belong to the king or even the kingdom? It might be where the king worships, but any true prophet would surely still claim these as God's sanctuary and temple. Clearly, Amaziah has decided that it makes sense for him, supposedly a prophet of God, to align himself with the rich and powerful. He has forgotten, or chosen to ignore, the fact that prophets are called by God to keep God's people in their covenant with God. Rather, he has chosen to follow the path of least resistance with those whom he recognizes as having political and economic power. He has decided that becoming a royal prophet is much better, more lucrative, easier than being a prophet of God. So, rather than challenge the status quo and remind the king and his court that they have a responsibility to rule justly and not to cheat the weak and poor, Amaziah, along with the other prophets, becomes part and parcel of that status quo. He is only too happy to tell the king what the king wants to hear about God's view of his rule, rather than fulfill his call to prophesy and call out the injustice and oppression he sees.

On the other hand, there is Amos, who is not even a member of the prophetic class. He is a farmer from Judah who heeds God's call to go and remind Israel whose people they were meant to be. He did not have the pedigreed access of the prophets found at court, but he had a commitment to God and to Israel's covenant with God. He could have stayed home, tried to keep his nose clean, and made a pretty good living. He did not have to challenge the leaders of Israel.

The Amaziahs of our day are all too obvious. We have religious leaders in almost all countries and political systems who throw in their lot with the rich and powerful. They are always shouting about keeping religion out of politics, when what they, like Amaziah, really mean is to keep out religion that makes the powerful uncomfortable. They are quite happy to talk about God placing leaders in power, or God blessing those with power or wealth. They are opposed to hearing the God who consistently, in both Hebrew and Christian Testaments, calls God's people to practice justice and act against injustice and oppression.

We see Amaziah in those religious leaders who preach a gospel of a God who blesses God's chosen with prosperity and power—those who teach that Christianity is all about getting as much as you can from the present economic dispensation. These are the most dramatic representations of the Amaziah school of Christianity, but threads of Amaziah can be seen even in those places that identify as progressive or liberal. It is the Amaziah tendency that has us not questioning the sources of the money we ask our parishioners to tithe. When churches and church leaders do not challenge members who make their money from private prisons or gun sales, we are leaning toward a Christianity that sits comfortably with the comfortable. When we select our vestries from those who are powerful, well-educated, professional, and respectable, we are leaning toward Amaziah's view of who we are meant to be as the church.

Clearly, this perspective has a great following in much of the world. It is these types of religious leaders who are most often seen and heard because they speak from the "king's sanctuary" and have the weight of the powers-that-be supporting them. There is a tendency to see them as the voice, face, and future of Christianity because they are so ubiquitous on all types of media. They are on TV, on social media, and in the newspapers, hawking their brand of Christianity as the future of the church. They are often personally wealthy. They build

We have religious leaders in almost all countries and political systems who throw in their lot with the rich and powerful.

huge sanctuaries that are regarded by many as the face of Christianity and they travel the world in their personal planes, proclaiming these material goods as a sign of God's pleasure in their words and actions. For many people, this is the future of Christianity: a faith and people who buy into the hierarchy of today, a faith that looks down on the poor and oppressed and sees them just as the world does—as something less than, as people of whom they can take further advantage.

This is not the future I want for our faith. I want our faith to be the other faith seen in our story, and I believe that I have seen this faith in many corners of the world, often hidden from the public eye. This is the faith of Amos.

When God calls Amos from his fairly stable life, Amos realizes that he is called to be in conflict with the prevailing wisdom and power structure of his day. Yet, he knows that he is called not simply to upbraid the people of Israel but to remind them who their God is and who they are called to be. It is not from hate or jealousy that Amos speaks out against Amaziah and the other royal prophets. Rather, it is from knowing that this is a people who have pledged themselves and their descendants to be in a covenantal relationship with God. The covenant is not about feast days or offering sacrifices to God; it is about how they are to live as a people in the world. They are meant to model a new way of being in community and to show that worshipping God is about every aspect of their lives.

Worship of God is not simply something we put on when we visit the temple. It is all about how we treat our neighbor, how we deal with the less fortunate, what we do to or for the widow and orphan, and how we treat the stranger in our midst. Amos tries to remind the people of Israel about this way of being and calls them back to it. For Amos, the call from God cannot be an opportunity to enrich himself or even to be one who lords it over those at the bottom of the political and economic ladder. His call is to make it clear to God's people

Our faith has never been about those who are most popular and those who preach prosperity.

that the God who created and loves them, expects that their belief in God will challenge them to live lives that mirror God's love. The God of Israel, the God whom we Christians claim is our God, wants those who worship in God's sanctuary to then go into the world and live that worship in their relationships with the rest of humanity and God's creation. This, then, is the faith that I believe can be the future of Christianity.

It is harder to see this Amos Christianity in the world, but I know it is there and I believe this is actually the more dominant story of Christianity. It is more hidden because it is not flashy or seeking attention in the way of Amaziah Christianity. I have seen it in the small parish of St. Thomas, Kagiso, South Africa. When we visited some years ago, the rector at the time, Xolani Dlwathi, told us, "We do not do outreach. Everything we do is worship." This congregation, comprised of predominantly poor families, fed lunch to children in the neighborhood school; bought school books, shoes, and uniforms for children in the community; stood as guardians for families of child-headed households; and made sure that those dying from AIDS had their homes cleaned, were eating healthy food, and knew they were loved. There was no fancy church sanctuary, no glamorous life for the rector, just worship of God that showed, through their caring, what Christianity is all about.

I have seen it at the Centro Kairos in Matanzas, Cuba, housed in a Baptist church, a place that offers clean water to the community, a space for children to learn how to play musical instruments, rooms where the lonely find relationships and a caring community, a place for women to make and sell their crafts—where all, no matter their denomination or faith tradition, can experience God's love through the hands and hearts of their neighbors.

I have seen it in the life of ministers like Janet Wolf, one of my spiritual mentors, who has consistently placed those who are caged in Tennessee at the center of her life and ministry. She shows us all that the incarcerated have a clear view of our justice system, can illustrate its flaws and failings, and offer us a new way of doing justice in the world. The sanctuaries in which she praises God are the detention centers and prisons.

Amos Christianity is Tami Forte Logan, an AME Zion pastor who knows that the struggle for racial and economic justice is a spiritual struggle and needs people of faith to step up and speak out. She has made it her life's work to call for an Amos Christianity from all those who profess the faith, founding and leading Faith4Justice in Western North Carolina.

I see the strength of an Amos Christianity in the works and words of Candice Benbow, a young public theologian who constantly calls the church to account for its abuses and failings, and models the life of a liberated Black Christian woman. Her Red Lip Theology speaks to a faith that is about our whole human experience.

There are days when I feel as though Amaziah Christianity is taking over my faith and I am despondent. It is easy to believe this is the case, especially in the United States, at a time when the voices lifted up as religious leaders are predominantly those of white men intent on maintaining their power and privilege. But, whenever I feel this way—without fail—I read a story, hear a sermon, see justice seekers, experience the power and commitment of Amos Christians like those I have named above. Then I am reminded that our faith has never been about those who are most popular and those who preach prosperity. It has been about the communities faithfully modeling a way of being in the world, of being in relationship with each other and with the prisoner and the hungry. It has been about voices reminding us that living God's love looks like our daily experiences. It has been about Amos, standing up to the establishment in the name of God and in the name of justice. So, I believe that the future of Christianity is indeed its past and present. It is Amos. It is us.   •

The Future of Christianity in a Global Context:

A Conversation with Wesley Granberg-Michaelson

By Shirin McArthur

Wesley Granberg-Michaelson is the author of *Future Faith: Ten Challenges Reshaping Christianity in the 21st Century*.

Shirin McArthur: Was there a particular incident or conversation that prompted you to write *Future Faith*?

Wesley Granberg-Michaelson: Good question. I had written a book called *From Times Square to Timbuktu: The Post-Christian West Meets the Non-Western Church*. The subtitle captures what I was trying to do: talk about the ways in which Christianity in the world is shifting, and also the impact of immigration on religious life in the United States.

But I felt, and others said, that I never fully explored what Christianity in the non-Western world really means for the historically established centers of Christianity, such as in the United States and Europe. While *Future Faith* wasn't a sequel, it really came out of that dialogue. People were saying to me, "I really like what you wrote. What comes next?"

So, I thought a lot about the kinds of challenges that are facing the future of Christianity and how that impacts US congregations, and that's what propelled me to write *Future Faith*.

Shirin: Which of the ten challenges do you think is most important for Western Christians to grasp or embrace, and why?

Wes: I've never been asked that, but I would say it's number three: Seeing through Non-Western Eyes. I think, in some ways, that's beneath a lot of the other challenges. It's this fundamental challenge of understanding that Christianity has now become predominantly a non-Western religion. It's moved out of the comfortable center of Western Enlightenment, dualistic thought, which was the cradle of Christianity for the last four hundred years. It now is becoming predominantly a non-Western religion, which means, if we relate to this as those who are shaped by Western culture, we have to understand what it really means to view the world in a different way, through what I call non-Western eyes.

Shirin: Your first chapter talks about the explosion of Christianity in the Global South and the need for American churches to be "liberated by a global story."[1] Your eighth challenge is entitled Defeating Divisive Culture Wars. Yet, when the Methodist Church met

The fundamental challenge is understanding that Christianity has now become predominantly a non-Western religion.

as a global body earlier this year, the cultural position of Christians from the Global South seemed to reject LGBTQIA+ Christians in America. How, then, do you see global churches helping to liberate American ones?

Wes: First, the church in the Global South does not have LGBTQIA+ issues at the top of its agenda. That's because the church in the Global South finds itself with existential questions of human survival: the basic issues of economic justice, the effects of climate change, the abuse of power. These are things that they feel immediately, in their context. They bring to the church in the West, so much that we can learn, from both their struggle and the persistence and vitality of their faith in the midst of so many difficult political, social, and economic pressures and circumstances.

So, I think it's a mistake, when we first look to the church in the Global South, to say, "Oh, yes, this is really interesting, the way this church is growing—but my gosh, the church in the Global South is so conservative on LGBTQIA+ issues now." It's true that the position of churches in the Global South, generally—and I want to stress *generally*—is very conservative on LGBTQIA+ issues. You saw that dynamic play out within the Methodist Church, but it's not uniformly so. Look at the church in South Africa, or look at people like Desmond Tutu.

I can take you to every continent where you can find, in the church, voices which are in a minority, but which are wanting to look at these questions through a different lens. You saw this just recently, where the high court of Botswana threw out laws on their books that were banning gay sex. Now, where did those laws come from? Those laws came from the British Empire. They are a legacy of colonialism. So, the whole picture becomes more complex than we commonly think.

Within Asian societies, within African societies, within Latino societies, if you go to the cultural level, you find a history of a variety of sexual practice—it's not often in the binary terms in which we place this, but that diversity is there.

Most of the church has taken a conservative view, but not all. When I say you need to be informed by the story of the church in the Global South, that doesn't mean that everyone is going to agree with everything that happens in the Global South, nor vice versa. It's a dialogue, and the division that I described in the eighth chapter, Defeating Divisive Culture Wars, this is going to be with us for the next thirty to forty years. It's not going away. No action by any general council or general synod is going to change anyone's sexual orientation. The underlying issue, in my view, is whether marriage is understood from the framework of covenant, or from biological difference. I think it's a covenant.

These issues will persist as divisions, both within the church in North America and within the global church. I think the question—which I tried to spell out in that chapter—is how we make sure that these differences are not ones which become dividing points in our fellowship. Let's not reach the point where we say, "Here's the line in the sand that determines who we are in fellowship with, in Christ, and who we're not," because I think that's the greatest danger. That's what I see happening within some denominations now.

Shirin: Speaking of dialogue, what's the most interesting conversation you've had about the book since it's been published?

Wes: When you write a book, if it's of any interest at all, you get speaking invitations. I got an invitation from the White Rock Baptist Church in Philadelphia. Their pastor, for decades, has been Dr. William Shaw. He's a friend of mine from ecumenical work and Christian Churches Together. This is a historic black church in Philadelphia, a thriving, strong, black Baptist church, one of importance in the city. It's the kind of church that every Democratic candidate for public office will want to come visit.

This invitation came, and I was delighted. Here's this white guy from the suburbs of Chicago, preaching to this strong black Baptist church. In the afternoon, they wanted me to give a lecture on the book and they had a reception, discussion, book signing, and so forth.

They were so appreciative and affirmative of this book, and it was a deep thrill, but I kept thinking about it. I think the reason why is that I wrote this book thinking mostly about global Christianity, but the message of the book is that the white, Western, and largely male rational way that has framed Christianity and its thought processes, its power structures, its outlook—that white bubble is now bursting. Movements around the world are demonstrating new voices, which have been more in the margins and are now coming to the center.

Well, I think those at White Rock Baptist Church heard that message, in terms of their own experience, and saw their witness as another example of what was happening globally. It put their story within the global story. I didn't write it with that framework in mind, but their response and their interpretation fit completely.

Shirin: Richard Rohr, in his article for this edition of *Oneing*, talks about his vision for "any future church" being "much flatter and much more inclusive." How does that vision interplay with your vision in *Future Faith*?

Wes: I think Richard's right. There are two things I particularly see in that regard. First is the importance of the growth of Pentecostalism throughout the world. Some background on Pentecostalism: It's only about 110 years old. In 1970, only 5 percent of Christians would identify as Pentecostal, but there's been a ten-fold growth, so that now, one out of every four Christians self-identifies as Pentecostal and Charismatic. It's one of the most important stories in the last century of Christianity.

Now, you have to ask what's going on there. In my view, it is a movement away from forms of Christian tradition that are highly rationalistic and highly structured, toward ways that build much more out of experience. When you say Pentecostal, it's very easy to have stereotypes and prejudices, but when you look at what's happening in Pentecostalism, especially in non-Western concepts, and see the growth in Pentecostal communities, especially amongst marginal groups, amongst the poor, Pentecostal style infuses much of the church. In other words, it's not simply limited to Pentecostal communities; you see that style infused in mainline and Catholic churches and so forth.

Pentecostalism, by its nature, moves toward a flatter, more inclusive way of practicing Christianity. A lot of Pentecostal denominations or groups have highly charismatic leaders and almost tribal ways. But, on the other hand, when you put the emphasis on experiential faith, you automatically undermine hierarchy.

That's where, when I think about what Richard says, and when I view what's happening in the global church—the emphasis on experiential faith, in all kinds of ways—and Richard himself has observed the connection between the contemplative tradition and a Pentecostal tradition. Many would think they are exact opposites, but they draw from a common foundation of religious experience. So, that's where I really see agreement with what Richard is hoping for.

At the same time, when you see the church growing in indigenous cultures, you also see the church taking on characteristic forms of those cultures, especially with regard to leadership.

I'll tell you a story. I was a member of the World Council of Churches Central Committee. I was sitting around a table with other members, and we introduced ourselves and talked. There was a church leader, Rufus Ositelu, from Africa, and we got talking. He's from the Church of the Lord Aladura, which no one in the West has ever heard of, because it's an African-instituted church, meaning the church formed in Africa, by Africans, rather than being formed by missionaries. There are many of these, and they're very important within the context of African Christianity.

So, he says, "We just finished an annual event—we have our leadership come together for prayer and fasting in August. We've always done this, since our founding, before we begin the new church year in the fall."

I say, "That's a great idea," and I was thinking that maybe we could learn from this.

Then he says, "On the weekend, we invite people from the wider church to come and gather with us for a festival."

I say, "That's a great idea. So, about how many people come when you do that?" And he says, "About one million."

Well, this August, I'm going to Nigeria to be at the Church of the Lord Aladura annual Tabieorah Festival, at his invitation.

Now, you look at a phenomenon like that and, on the one hand, you'll find His Holiness Primate Rufus Ositelu, he is the leader of that worldwide church. He is regarded almost like a pope. So, the pattern of leadership, I think it fits within the African cultural context. At the same time, the power of these churches to welcome and include and, frankly, empower those who belong is extraordinary. These are stories that are typical of what happens in the church in Africa, which is just hard for us in the West to really comprehend.

Shirin: It sounds like you would be ultimately optimistic about the future of Christianity.

Wes: Oh, I am. All you have to do is look at the stories, look at the statistics, look at what's happening globally. While Christianity in its non-Western expressions is taking many different forms, and you have lots of challenges and issues, you have forms of Christianity that are almost ahistorical. They haven't much connection to the tradition of the church—to the "church catholic," the broader, global church—but they are filled with enormous spiritual vitality.

They are mainly within the communities of those who are marginalized. They are exhibiting expressions of faith that are integrated and holistic. They're not dominated by the kinds of "evangelism on

I think there are deep questions about the future of Christianity in the United States. There are *not* questions about the future of Christianity in the world.

the one hand and social justice on the other," those silly dichotomies in the church in the West. They see Christianity as a whole. These expressions, in their spiritual commitment and vitality, point to a very strong future.

I think the only question is whether the church in the West, and the church in the United States, are going to be a part of this future or whether it will increasingly diminish and falter. Only one congregation in ten in the US reflects the demographic of people between the ages of nineteen and thirty-five in the US.

You have those challenges, plus whether the non-white expressions of the church will really be embraced, and whether the church can move out of the kind of frozen, dualistic mindset that Richard has been writing about for so many years.

I think there are deep questions about the future of Christianity in the United States. There are *not* questions about the future of Christianity in the world.

Shirin: Is there anything else your heart is feeling called to share on this topic?

Wes: Thinking about the other themes that are in *Future Faith*, I think of number nine: Belonging before Believing. I think that also gets to the heart of so much about where Christianity is and where it's going, and it relates a lot, as well, to Richard's work, and those at the Center for Action and Contemplation.

We are caught in this paradigm of: You come to some intellectual assent that causes you to say, "I believe in this," and it gets captured either in a creed or in some formulation, and then you decide, "Well, I'm going to join a church." Then that church becomes a bounded set that is defined by how it draws the boundaries, the fences around itself, as opposed to experiences of the church. This was really brought to light by Paul Hiebert, an anthropologist and missionary in India, who said, "Here, you belong to community first, as you then try to clarify what you believe."

I think that kind of paradigm, that reversal, strikes at the heart of how so much of the church in our own Western culture is structured and organized, and assumes and understands itself. The book I'm working on now is centered on pilgrimage. The reason I like it so much is that I believe we have to walk our way into faith, to get a hold of what it means to reverse that normal paradigm for understanding the community and understanding how we believe. That's, again, something that the church in the Global South has to teach us, and I think that presents one of our deeper challenges.

Here's another thing. When I give talks about the book, the most frequently cited example that people will share with me afterward is the question of how you herd cattle in Australia. It gets exactly at this question: Do you build a fence, or do you build a well? •

RECOMMENDED READING

The Future of Wisdom:
Toward a Rebirth of Sapiential Christianity

Bruno Barnhart
Monkfish, 2018

A Book Review by Lee Staman

In his book *The Future of Wisdom: Toward a Rebirth of Sapiential Christianity*, Bruno Barnhart (1931–2015), a monk of the New Camaldoli Hermitage, sought to do exactly what the subtitle suggests. The introduction is a whirlwind race through two thousand years of the Christian wisdom tradition along with a brief epistemic grounding in perennial philosophy. I would have liked to see at least a brief footnote pointing out that while the wisdom tradition in the West dimmed after the thirteenth century, the Eastern Orthodox Church continued deeper developments in this area.

The first of four movements begins with what he called "The Sapiential Awakening." Cynthia Bourgeault captures the sense of the word *sapiential* in the foreword to this second edition by pointing out that sapiential does what "wisdom" or "non-dual" cannot: point to a living tradition, "a sacred stream of spiritual transmission that was being dynamically lived and handed on."[1] Barnhart's first movement focuses on recapturing the Christian wisdom tradition as it appears especially in Karl Rahner and Thomas Merton.

The second movement, "The Eastern Turn," looks at sapiential wisdom from the East, especially focusing on its non-dual characteristics. While drawing attention to Hindu, Taoist, and Buddhist concepts, Barnhart really seemed to favor Hindu insights over the other two.

The third movement, "The Western (Modern) Turn," returns to the West and Barnhart did well to break down the past five hundred years, highlighting the move toward modernity and individualism. A word of warning: It is possible to get lost in the second and third movements. There is a lot of technical language and it can be difficult to follow the thought process and arguments, but it is worth pursuing, especially if you are unfamiliar with the content.

I will say that the fourth movement, "The Global (Postmodern) Turn," is where this book came alive for me. Here Barnhart reached his goal of incarnational wisdom: "We can look at the entire historical process as an *incarnation of divine Wisdom in the whole of humanity*."[2] The arguments of the fourth movement were clear and his critiques spot-on. He also had the self-awareness to know the shortcomings of his endeavor: "We have said little of the Holy Spirit, little of woman, or the feminine, and little of the human psyche and its intuitive knowing. A serious exploration . . . would require another book."[3]

The book ends with an essay written by Cyprian Consiglio in memoriam of Barnhart. He does a beautiful job of fleshing out how Barnhart saw the cross as a four-part mandala: the first movement is the Silence represented by God the Creator, the second movement is the Word/Jesus Christ, the third is Music/Spirit, and the fourth is Dance/Incarnation (*kenosis*). This was a profound view of the cross for me and I thank Barnhart for it.

Overall, I found this book wanting in some areas but more than enough to ponder in others. For anyone interested in wisdom traditions and recovering a different facet of Christian spirituality, *The Future of Wisdom* would be worth investigating.   •

NOTES

On the Mystery of the Incarnation

1 Denise Levertov, "On the Mystery of the Incarnation," *The Stream & The Sapphire: Selected Poems on Religious Themes* (New York: New Directions, 1997), 19.

Christianity's Future: An Evolutionary Perspective

1 Ilia Delio, *The Unbearable Wholeness of Being: God, Evolution, and the Power of Love* (Maryknoll, NY: Orbis, 2013), xvi, 98. Like other contemporary Christian scholars reclaiming a spiritual meaning for evolution, Ilia Delio draws heavily on the vision of Teilhard de Chardin. John F. Haught, Elizabeth A. Johnson, and Ursula King are among other significant exponents.

2 This approach I have outlined in detail in my book, *Ancestral Grace: Meeting God in Our Human Story* (Maryknoll, NY: Orbis, 2008) and in abbreviated form in *Beyond Original Sin: Recovering Humanity's Creative Urge* (Maryknoll, NY: Orbis, 2018). It supplements rather than contradicts the more expansive vision outlined by Richard Rohr in his recent book, *The Universal Christ: How a Forgotten Reality Can Change Everything We See, Hope For, and Believe* (New York: Convergent, 2019).

3 One of the finest studies on the archetypal significance of Jesus is that of Walter Wink, *The Human Being: Jesus and the Enigma of the Son of Man* (Minneapolis: Augsburg Fortress, 2002).

4 The language used by theologian Peter C. Hodgson in *Winds of the Spirit: A Constructive Christian Theology* (Louisville, KY: Westminster John Knox, 1994), 232.

5 Learn more in my books *Christianity's Dangerous Memory: A Rediscovery of the Revolutionary Jesus* (New York: Crossroad, 2011) and *On Being a Postcolonial Christian: Embracing an Empowering Faith* (self-pub., CreateSpace, 2014).

6 As outlined in Rohr, *The Universal Christ*.

7 The approach adopted by Richard Rohr in *The Divine Dance: The Trinity and Your Transformation* (New Kensington, PA: Whitaker House, 2016).

8 More on these two developments in my book *In the Beginning Was the Spirit: Science, Religion, and Indigenous Spirituality* (Maryknoll, NY: Orbis, 2012).

Abide in Me: The Church's Love Affair with Christ

1 John R. Quinn, *Ever Ancient, Ever New: Structures of Communion in the Church* (Mahwah, NJ: Paulist, 2013), 3.

2 Ibid., 1.

3 Reginald H. Fuller and Daniel Westberg, *Preaching the Lectionary: The Word of God for the Church Today*, 3rd ed. (Collegeville, MN: Liturgical Press, 2006), 479.

4 Iain Matthew, *The Impact of God: Soundings from St. John of the Cross* (London: Hodder & Stoughton, 1995), 46.

5 Ibid.

6 Jean-Pierre de Caussade, *Abandonment to Divine Providence*, trans. John Beevers (New York: Image, 1975), 36.

7 James Joyce, *Finnegans Wake* (Ware, UK: Wordsworth Editions, 2012), 32.

8 Pope Paul VI, *Lumen Gentium*, November 21, 1964, I:1, http://www.vatican.va/archive/hist_councils/ii_vatican_council/documents/vat-ii_const_19641121_lumen-gentium_en.html.

9 de Caussade, *Abandonment to Divine Providence*, 113.

10 John of the Cross, "The Living Flame of Love," Stanza 4, trans. Marjorie Flower, as quoted in Matthew, *The Impact of God*, 24.

Powering Down: The Future of Institutions

1 University of New Mexico School of Medicine, "Project ECHO: A Revolution in Medical Education and Care Delivery," https://echo.unm.edu/.

2 Paulo Freire, *Pedagogy of the Oppressed: 50th Anniversary Edition*, trans. Myra Bergman Ramos (New York: Bloomsbury Academic, 2018), 38, 39.

3 See Jonathan Wilson-Hartgrove, *Reconstructing the Gospel: Finding Freedom from Slaveholder Religion* (Downers Grove, IL: IVP Books, 2018).

4 See Joe Holland, *Roman Catholic Clericalism: Three Historical Stages in the Legislation of a Non-Evangelical, Now Dysfunctional, and Sometimes Pathological Institution* (Washington, DC: Pacem in Terris Press, 2018).

Loving the Church Back to Life

1 As quoted in Paul Francis Lanier, *No Love So Sure: The Book* (Maitland, FL: Xulon Press, 2003), 99.

2 Jelani Cobb, "William Barber Takes on Poverty and Race in the Age of Trump," *New York Times*, May 7, 2018, https://www.newyorker.com/magazine/2018/05/14/william-barber-takes-on-poverty-and-race-in-the-age-of-trump.

3 You can sign this pledge at https://www.redletterchristians.org/pledge/.

4 Edward Mote, "My Hope Is Built on Nothing Less," 1834.

5 If you're looking for some great leaders and writers, check out https://www.redletterchristians.org/people/.

The Future of Christianity in a Global Context: A Conversation with Wesley Granberg-Michaelson

1 Wesley Granberg-Michaelson, *Future Faith: Ten Challenges Reshaping Christianity in the 21st Century* (Minneapolis: Fortress, 2018), 20.

The Future of Wisdom: Toward a Rebirth of Sapiential Christianity

1 Bruno Barnhart, *The Future of Wisdom: Toward a Rebirth of Sapiential Christianity* (Rhinebeck, NY: Monkfish, 2018), xi.

2 Ibid., 195.

3 Ibid., 198.

Coming Spring 2020!

Liminal Space, Vol. 8, No. 1

The Spring 2020 edition of *Oneing* will address "Liminal Space," a term that refers to a space or time on the threshold between what has been and what is to come. Often brought on by great suffering or great love, a period of liminality can support a person during a much-needed transition—in some cases from the first half of life to the second half of life.

Examples of transitions brought on during this liminal period include a painful divorce; the loss of a beloved family member, friend, or pet; falling in love; the birth of a child; or a *metanoia* or conversion experience.

Contributors to this edition of *Oneing* include Teddy Carney (1927–2015), a dear friend of Richard Rohr who gifted the CAC with its main campus at 1705 Five Points Road; Anne and Terry Symens-Bucher, founders of Canticle Farm—an urban farm, educational center, and intentional community experimenting at the intersections of faith-based, social-justice-based, and Earth-based nonviolent activism; and Richard Rohr.

Both the limited-print edition of CAC's literary journal,
Oneing, and the downloadable PDF version
will be available for sale in April 2020
at https://store.cac.org/.

Center for
Action and
Contemplation

A collision of opposites forms the cross of Christ.
One leads downward preferring the truth of the humble.
The other moves leftward against the grain.
But all are wrapped safely inside a hidden harmony:
One world, God's cosmos, a benevolent universe.